THE
POACHER'S HANDBOOK

THE
POACHER'S
HANDBOOK

IAN NIALL

Illustrated
with wood engravings by

BARBARA GREG

Foreword by
BERNARD O'DONOGHUE

Merlin Unwin Books

Published by

Merlin Unwin Books
Palmers House
7 Corve Street
Ludlow
Shropshire SY8 1DB
U.K.

Tel: 01584 877456   Fax: 01584 877457

First published in Great Britain by William Heinemann in 1950
Published by White Lion Books in 1992
Reprinted 1992, 1994, 1997, 2000, and 2001
This edition published by Merlin Unwin Books, 2002
Reprinted 2005

The publishers are grateful to Marian Janes for her help in lending some
of Barbara Greg's original wood engravings and for her support.
Additional design by Clare Byatt.

ISBN 1 873674 589

Printed and bound in Great Britain by CPI Bath

DEDICATED TO SUCH CHARACTERS AS

FRANCIE McGINN
BUTCHER MURPHY
SNIB, BLACK BILL
AND LITTLE HUGH

MASTERS ALL

AND

*for the man with the hare-pocket
and the boy with the snare*

IAN NIALL is the author of eleven novels and many books on country matters including *Pastures New* and *Fresh Woods*. In 1990 he celebrated forty years as a columnist, beginning with *The Spectator* and then *Country Life*, where he is known and loved by a wide public for his regular contributions to 'A Countryman's Notes'. He was born in Scotland and he spent his formative years on his grandfather's farm in Wigtownshire, recalled in *A Galloway Childhood*. Married with three grown up children and five grandchildren, he and his wife now live in the Chilterns after more than forty years in Wales.

BARBARA GREG was born at Styal, Cheshire in 1900. She studied at the Slade School and the Central School of Art where she learnt wood engraving, and at Westminster School of Art. She married Norman Janes in 1925, also a wood engraver. Some of Barbara Greg's earliest designs were for book endpapers printed from wood and lino-cuts. All her book illustrations depict scenes from nature and the countryside. She became a member of the Society of Wood Engravers in 1952. Books illustrated by her include *A Fisherman's Log* by G. L. Ashley-Dodd. *Enigmas of Natural History* and *More Enigmas of Natural History* by E. L. Grant Watson, *Fresh Woods* and *Pastures New*, both by Ian Niall. She died in 1983.

BERNARD O'DONOGHUE was born in Cullen in the rural depths of North Cork in 1945. He moved to Manchester in 1962 and since 1965 he has lived in Oxford where he teaches English at Magdalen College. He has written on medieval English, as well as four books of poetry: *Razorblades and Pencils* (1984); *Poaching Rights* (1987); *The Absent Signifier* (1990); *The Weakness* (1991). His wife Heather is a scholar of Old Norse; they have three children.

FOREWORD

by Bernard O'Donoghue

ANYONE who has ever had a tooth filled is familiar with Ian Niall's 'A Countryman's Notes' from *Country Life,* traditionally the only pleasure associated with visits to the dentist. The reader of those Notes is never in any doubt about being in the presence of a master of his art. In the preface to *The Poacher's Handbook,* Ian Niall says of poaching 'no great art dies'. This is at least as true of writing as of any other art. This book is the triumph of the poacher turned writer, by a master of both crafts.

The Poacher's Handbook is a classic essay in one of the major sub-genres in English Literature, the naturalist's diary or handbook. Since Walton's *The Compleat Angler,* it has been a form that breaks down solemn distinctions between serious and entertaining writing. It is a long and distinguished heritage, embracing Gilbert White, John Clare, Kilvert and Flora Thompson. Further afield it has philosophical echoes in Thoreau. All of these works have two things in common, both pre-eminently present in the writings of Ian Niall: they are perfectly written, and they are unfailingly interesting to read. The complaint is often made these days, not without reason, that the most interesting writers are not the most praised. Ian Niall is guilty here, being deficient in both obscurity and pretension; no reader will fall asleep over *The Poacher's Handbook.*

As for the writerly skills, they are evident in every paragraph: the line of every sentence is let out to the right length and tension. These are the skills, maybe, more associated with the good poet than the prose narrator, in the way the particularity of the individual experience is made to evoke a general truth. The wisdom of the poacher is the same as of any other practitioner of life. The novice poacher is warned against going over the old paths too often because "it is habit that makes it possible to catch the hare, and a regular pattern of behaviour is the thing that brings a poacher to the dock".

vii

Ian Niall's mythic poaching is placeless as well as ageless. It is taken from the Wigtownshire of his childhood and the North Wales of his adulthood, but its locale is anywhere outdoors. It is the same with the unforgettable characters who people these pages. They are not only individuals carved attentively from memory: they are universal figures too, in the line of Falstaff and Autolycus and Mr Jingle. You and I are not personally acquainted with Little Hugh; but we would recognise him if we did meet him, skulking in his old raincoat, waiting patiently for the main, or the half chance. Francie McGinn is another skilful character; Butcher Murphy bides his time at the corner. These are the mythic figures to whom this book is dedicated. It is not a dedication that is lightly earned.

No writing, whatever its subject or however unportentous its air, can be excellent without an ethical sense. Here this is lightly carried, but Ian Niall is a writer you trust from the first. This is part of the reason why you don't remain satisfied with half a dozen readings of this *Poacher's Handbook* but will want to move on to his other books: to the marvellous memoir, *A Galloway Childhood*, the confessions of an addicted fly-fisherman, *Trout From the Hills*, or the philosopher-ornithologist in *Feathered Friends*.

We cannot say where critical posterity will place these finely turned books. It may be that it will find more humanity and truth in them than in the currently most celebrated fiction. What we can say is that *The Poacher's Handbook* is a classic contribution to a tradition of secure masterpieces in the history of English, and that there are not many contemporary works that we can place with such confidence.

All the classics of this form have had their engravers. Here the original wood engravings of Barbara Greg display a blend of evocativeness and verisimilitude that entirely suits their text. Look at the trout-tickler or the humourously, darkly sinister poacher or the cameos of lake and mountain scenes. These illustrations catch beautifully a world both in and beyond history, this utopia of animals and people.

OXFORD, *July 1992*

AUTHOR'S NOTE

IN 1950, when this book was first published, I wrote by way of introduction:

> There is perhaps no better way of studying an art than examining the technique of the masters, and the student will find in this modest work portraits of men whose art has been recognised by authority; men who have devoted their lives to the subject, suffered severe penalties in the dogged pursuit of their calling - fines up to five pounds and many days in prison.
>
> Poaching is said to be a dying art, but I do not believe this. No great art dies. Congenital poachers will father poachers. It is an old thing. Hunting is in the blood. So long as there is a warren to shelter a rabbit, a holly bush in which a bird roosts and a hollow or a hill for a hare, there will be a man or boy who will put his natural cunning to stalking the hare, hunting the wild thing, and outwitting both the quarry and the representative of authority.

Nearly half a century later, it is a great pleasure to see the original *The Poacher's Handbook* with Barbara Greg's wood engravings available once more.

When I first had the idea of 'a handbook for the man with a hare pocket and the boy with a snare', I knew it would need a very good illustrator, someone with the touch of Thomas Bewick, and certainly, if there were to be wood engravings, someone with a particular feeling for the natural scene. The choice of the publisher was Barbara Greg and I have always felt I was particularly fortunate in having such a gifted artist to illustrate not only *The Poacher's Handbook* but the two other titles that followed, *Fresh Woods* and *Pastures New*. Barbara had to be supplied with one or two props in the shape of rabbit snares and a gin trap and I don't think she had set many snares around her family home in Cheshire. I was delighted with the drafts she sent me and enchanted by her finished engravings, pulls of four of which hang in my house today.

Our collaboration was something that should have been carried on, but for some reason the publisher wanted change. A revised edition called *The New Poacher's Handbook* was published. It contained a few more bits and pieces that didn't add to the artistry or literary merit of the original, and a different illustrator was selected. There is a world of difference between something that comes flashing from a writer's mind and something that is amended or refurbished. The first was inspired, if anything I have written was, and Barbara Greg's illustrations have always seemed to me to be just right for this book. I cannot help wondering what might have been had my early association with the particularly gifted artist had been allowed to flourish. Belatedly I salute her.

ASHLEY GREEN *July 1992*

A MAN named Jeck was my first teacher. If he is still alive I imagine he is less nimble and even more astute than when I was his pupil at five years of age. Jeck worked for us to the annoyance of neighbours who had game on their land. He was unreliable as a worker. One day he would be at the plough, plodding the hill with the gulls flying behind him and the next day he would be missing. From our biggest hill, a hog's back topped by a fir planting, most of the countryside could be seen. Jeck could see the river; the little woods, that clogged the hollows, ran along lesser hills and stretched back into the moss. Sometimes I stumbled and staggered up to the plough with his tea-can and buttered scones and he would crouch on his heels, take a mouthful of tea, and look dreamily at the landscape to the west.

I

"Johnnie boy," he would say, "see yonder? It's the greatest place for an old cock pheasant. I seen the day when I could walk quiet along yon hedgeside, slip through the fence an' let fly."

And the next day Jeck would be missing. Perhaps I would hear that he had seen such a day again, but I was a very small boy, and small boys are rarely the recipients of confidences that might put a man in prison.

Before the schoolmaster, who needed a strap to inculcate knowledge, had conveyed the sequence of the alphabet to my brain, Jeck had given me the way of straightening snare wire, forming the pear-shaped noose, yes, and the vital intelligence of the setting height and the place in which to set. I put down my first snare under Jeck's supervision. It was on a stubble slope where a hare was running at night. When the alarm awoke the household for the five o'clock milking, long before the grey streak of early winter dawn and the first cock-crow from the locked henhouse, I was out of bed. The frost bit my toes. I could not wait to put on stockings and lace my little boots. I had to go barefoot and half-dressed, as I often did in summer. I crossed the field, skirted the gloomy clumps of gorse and ducked under the squealing fence to come to the hillside. Before I saw my catch I could hear the thump of his powerful back legs as he bounded in the noose. I ran to him, clasped him in my arms, drew the pin and carried him homeward, while every wild kick lacerated my bare knees.

Many years later, returning from school in the south, I had the opportunity of fishing a stretch of salmon water owned by a neighbour, a privilege obtained for me by my aunts, who wanted to keep me out of disreputable company for as long as I could be diverted. I went with borrowed net and gaff, borrowed flies and a rod like a binder whip. A whole afternoon I cast and re-cast my flies, and when the village school spilled its children on the road I was joined by a torn-trousered urchin. He unwound a length of twine to which he attached a clumsy hook. On the hook he fastened a piece of red flannel, snipped, perhaps, from his grandmother's petticoat, and cast hook and red bait into the water. In five minutes he had a pike on his line. It careered this way and that. The water swirled and gave up bubbles and the boy hastened to a stump, round which he looped his line. I watched, fascinated, while he brought the long-snouted, fierce-looking gad-fish to the bank, and then I wound up my reel, put the delicate cast back in the pouch and went home. Someone had told me when I was quite small that the way to catch a salmon was to put a prawn on a hook, use salmon roe, draw a net, or hook him out of the water at the salmon-leap, and the way to catch a pike was to use red flannel; bait a hook with a live frog, or even a mouse.

Put the conventional behind you. Put your hand in the horny palm of Francie McGinn and come to the stable to learn the knots for net-making. Look now and then at the silvery light of the moon on the cobwebbed skylight and know that this is a night for staying at home, for the moon is too full and the ground too hard and the night too still. Talk small and listen to a thing as old as the hills, as natural as the gentle swish of the fir branches, the raindrops spearing across a deep pool.

The ways of coming by a rabbit, a pheasant, partridge or trout are as numerous as the hairs on your

mongrel dog. You must learn the use of the gate net, the long net, the snare, the ferret, the purse net and many other devices from a whistle to a kite. You must learn to walk softly and to listen long, when to run and when to stand still; the thing to do in the black hat of night and the way to read the flushed magpie and the laugh of the jay. A pigeon in flight never crosses directly over a man on open ground. When a faraway pigeon deviates in the line of flight you must learn to watch for the subsequent movement of sheep from the hedge to the corner of the field and the horse's pricked ears. It is wrong to go hastily away like the startled partridge rising among your feet. Close at hand is the hawthorn hedge, the clump of hazels and the shadows that swallow you from the bright light of the day.

You will hear every way of finding game and every

4

trick in taking fish. Legends there are too, ways that are not practised but only talked about, because they are cruel or outlandish.

Francie McGinn and I will take you across the moss where the grey hen is feeding. We will not walk with the bullock-stagger of a shooting party with beaters and luncheon baskets. For a long time we will stand in the shelter of the drystone wall, close by the nodding gorse, watching the sheep out of sight over the heather slope. When they are gone you and I will walk slowly with Francie. Watch him. He is like that old drawing of the disreputable character with the gun. Not quite the sporting gentleman, because he does not need a beater to show him where the birds sit. He has taken an interest in birds and the moor. He did not step from a panelled dining-hall to a gun-room after port last night. We will move across the peat diggings and the waterholes. The birds will rise and whirr away. Francie will thrust his gun at them and one will fall. The brown bog hare will flatten his ears and race over a rise and three snipe skim and arc out of sight. When we are back in the cover of the willow clump, men with glasses will scan the moss for us; watching the sheep for frightened movement, listening for the betraying cry of the cursed curlew.

It is not a new thing. It is old, old like the scent of peat smoke from the lonely cottage; the cairn on the hill; the flight of geese in late October. In the flat country of East Anglia a man rose at five to-day to take a pheasant, and last night, in Wiltshire, kindred spirits were running out the long net, stopping to recognise the yelp of the fox and the cry of the owl.

THE hare runs the grass hill and sleeps in a fold
of ground in a bed as snug, as sheltered, as that of the
little field mouse. Here a clump of hay-brown grass
stands alone and conspicuous, but you can see through
it. You can see the contour of the ground with its
ridges of a past season's ploughing where the vetch
and yarrow grow. The grass tops sway a little in the
earth-close breeze and are still again. Summer has
gone and no grasshopper sings. Right in the middle
of the clump of grass lies the hare. His haunches are
raised and his ears smooth on his neck. He is soft
brown, darker brown, matched to the grass, its seeds
more silvery at the tips; matched to the ground,
every beautiful hair a blend with the surroundings.
He sleeps in the warmth of the October or late
September noon.

6

The scents of the field soothe him, and the senses of the hunter are drugged by the breath of the land, the scents of decay, of dying leaves and mushroom growth, by the very beauty of the shades of feeble autumn, the little red fungus on the fragment of twig, the stubble bleaching fawn. This one is the hare of the arable fields. The one from the bogs seems taller of leg and darker. When he rears among the round rushes, pausing on the patch of hair grass to take a message from the wind, he seems a bigger animal. As he moves in through the rushes he retains that impression of stature. The hare of the mountain is certainly smaller. He is grey and has a tinge of blue. He reminds those who see him of blots of frozen snow up where the air is cold and the streams are sheathed in a covering of ice. They are all wild, the hare of the rough wet hollows, the hare of the clover hill and the hare of the cold mountain, wild like the cry of the peewit and the sad and lonely flight of the heron.

One will have his sleeping place on the southern slope of a distant hill, and another in the wood where the bracken has folded upon itself in a clearing. Their movement out of wood or across the brow will be a thing so graceful that when you see it for the first time you will stand and stare long after they are gone. You will not often get close enough to see the hare in his form. He will be gone while you clamber the dry-stone wall and bring loose stones about your heels. His long back legs will take him fast across the hollow, the shadow of a wind-driven cloud, through the gap and away, running easily for the meadow and the shelter of the longer grass. When you have steadied

7

your heartbeat and brushed the grey moss of the stones from your flanks you will walk past the spot where he sleeps from mid-morn until afternoon. It will be warm with the heat of his fur and if you come and disturb it with your fumbling hands it is likely that to-morrow he will sleep elsewhere at noon, so it is as well, perhaps, that you are blind to such things.

Yonder he runs on the skyline. See him speeding for the march fence. In the early morning he will be

back across the grass field, feeding in the first gold shafts of sunlight that break above the horizon. When you walk the stubble, undulating over the ground of summer's harvest, you will look up to see him going like a bird. It is the poetry of action one sees in the bounding deer, the blood horse, yes, and, in its way, the stoat, hot after his prey. Evening, and he comes bobbing down the furrow. Now he halts to take stock of the countryside or, as you or I, admire the sunset and the far-away blue shadows that hang to the woods and make the ragged mountains look restful.

There is no need for pity. He has a strong heart and

a body to carry him to the steepest hilltop. He has sensitive ears and back legs with power enough to snap the woven wire of the snare, unless the poacher uses cunning. You may walk with your gun to catch him asleep in the morning when the watery sunlight is like a dying fire in the east. Down wind you may walk, knowing no better. You may walk softly with every sense alert. The wind blows through the thorn tree, rocking the dead thistle and shrivelled dock, taking the hot breath from your lips. The dead leaves roll through the dried stalks and at every stride you feel the bite of winter making your ears tingle, and gnawing at your cheeks. Across the sleeping field to halt at the dyke. When you turn it will be to see him flying for the gate, going fast into the wind like a pigeon. All your natural cunning was not enough. You have something to learn from Francie McGinn and Little Hugh and Black Bill.

IF you value the opinion of the ladies of the village you will stay respectable. Old Mrs. Barret will nod her head in approval and say, "Good steady man, is John. Not like some I know, always at the poaching and getting up before the Bench."

You will put away from you all thought of a night with the long net and sleep snug in bed. When the wind cries round the eaves and a spattering of rain goes over the window above the well of the stairs, you will turn drowsily and listen for the clock chiming the half-hour and perhaps think that had you been less of a good steady man, like those in the churchyard, you might have been walking over a carpet of fir and pine needles, pondering the shadow in the tree.

If you care nothing for respectability and, after all, respectability is in the mouths of the old women a thing relative to the strength of the latest piece of gossip, you may find the policeman less friendly and the gamekeeper making dark threats in the public bar. Have courage.

"I got my eye on him," he will say. "Thinks I don't know. I'm just waitin' my time. I don't want no slip-ups. I want him an' his friends to get sent up the line."

Under such threats I lived happily and quite safely for many a season. Have no fear of his talk. He talks that way to have an excuse for his lack of wits. He hopes you will hear and be frightened. Of course he waits his time. We all wait our time. Live and let live. He is paid to catch you and but for you he might be out of work.

In Wales they speak affectionately of the "old poachers" being about again. "Look, there he goes," someone will nudge his neighbour. "Biggest old poacher for miles round. If ever you want a hare, he's the man. He's got them counted better than the keeper!" Become a poacher and they will smile every time your name is mentioned. The tenant farmers, especially those with mean landlords, too jealous of their rights and slow to carry out repairs, will close their eyes to a hurried walk through the wood and across the meadow at dusk. The bigger farmers will be distant and perhaps hostile, and the landlord, once his keeper has pointed you out to him, will look at you with acute distaste, hoping that one of his neighbours will have you before him in the prisoner's dock at Monday's court.

"Trespassing in pursuit of game," the clerk will say,

and the magistrate will frown, purse his lips and clear his throat.

"You have done a bad thing. It is wrong indeed and there is a punishment. You deserve punishment too, for you have been caught. The law will make you understand that you must not trespass in pursuit of game. You must not be caught again or you will go to prison."

Did you see the little man in the back row? He was grey-haired and had a coloured rag tied at his throat. He was wearing corduroy trousers and an over-large jacket. His eyes were very innocent. He sympathises and shares your indignation at the injustice of your disqualification from holding a gun licence. Why, only twelve months ago he was fined ten pounds and he had no more than two rabbits in his possession when he was caught. Of course, circumstances were different. It took luck to catch Little Hugh. He didn't net his first burrow yesterday. He looks into the tree in the dark, and he knows the roosting crow from the roosting pheasant. His was a case of hard luck, and luck is a thing no one can pop into his bag when he lifts his ferret from its box.

Little Hugh gathers mushrooms and firewood. It enables him to watch and take note. He does a bit of hedging and ditching. He can manage an isolated burrow with three nets and a ferret while he is trimming and bending the sticks of the hedge. The ferret travels in his jacket pocket, as tame as the old spinster's cat. Little Hugh can take his old gun along with his ditching tools, the sickle, the mattock, the draining shovel and the hedge-knife. If the pheasant, feeding where the old corn stack once stood, ventures a little nearer the ditch, Hugh will take one shot after he has stared idly around for ten minutes or so. He can move very fast for a man of sixty. Up out of the ditch, through the wire and over to the bird and back almost before the echo has returned from the hill.

Someone comes down the field, suspicious of Little Hugh, perhaps, but the pheasant is on the bank covered by a tangle of green weed, blackberry and uprooted cress. A shot? Surprise at finding someone standing so close shows on Little Hugh's face. Yes, he heard a shot not long ago and wondered about it too. Is the keeper on his rounds? Who could be shooting at this time of day? The old gun is lying down in the ditch, balanced on three stones close to the bank. Stand clear. Small pebbles and marshy grit come swinging up on the shovel. A dog is barking the cows home. Little Hugh adjusts his cap and feels in the farthest corner of his buttonless waistcoat's pocket. When the stump of cigarette is smouldering in his sheltering palm he calls to the departing visitor. Is it nearly tea time?

Before you learn to catch a hare, let me introduce you to Little Hugh and say at once that the introduction is worth no more than my standing with this great poacher. One can know such men for a long time without being invited to share their company after game.

When Little Hugh was at school he had snare-wire in his pocket and a bit of a pied dog that waited for him at the gate until he went home at night. Poaching was in his blood. Someone taught him to cut snare pegs and the ways of getting a rabbit before he had left school. At the end of his schooldays his father got him a job in the garden of the big house, but it went wrong. At that time they kept peacocks. These magnificent birds strutted the lawns and swept through the paths that were hedged by little shrubs. The gardener's boy was fascinated. He thought it would be wonderful to have one about the cottage door at home, a thing his mother could admire as she sat in the doorway peeling potatoes and keeping her eye on the smaller children. Who has not tried to carry away beauty? The taking of the peacock became a thing upon which Little Hugh set his heart and his wits. How would you catch a peacock? Run at it, embrace it and carry it away down a broad drive and across a wide tree-dotted park with every blade of grass the same height and not a shadow of cover? Could you hide a peacock and walk home with it along five winding miles of quiet road?

One afternoon the boy put the dregs of a whisky bottle on a picking of chicken meal and laid it on the flags of the path, keeping watch from the herb plot

14

where he made pretence of working with a hoe. The peacock came. Its beak darted at the drops of meal. In a little while the bird was stupefied and Hugh quickly tied a sugar bag on its head. For the rest of the afternoon the peacock sat in drunken contemplation under a laurel bush. Could he have some geranium cuttings? begged Little Hugh. The under-gardener considered and then gave his consent. The peacock left the grounds in a sack from which geranium cuttings protruded through a conspicuous hole.

The grand bird was released in the garden of the cottage. It was ruffled and bedraggled, with no tail display. Little Hugh hastened to inform his mother. The children clustered behind her as she stood on the step, staring at the peacock in horror. The uproar had hardly reached its peak when the head gardener descended from a gig. There was a stern look on his face. The peacock, which had been ignored by the family, had had the attention of a dog and had been chased through a hole in the hedge. It looked no better than a hen-pecked bantam. The gamekeeper, who came to know Little Hugh much better in time, rounded it up and put it back in the sack. The head gardener delivered a lecture during which he brandished a stick. Finally he bade Little Hugh farewell.

Shortly afterwards Hugh was caught on the lawn of the big house. He had a rod and line with which he had been trying to lure the giant old carp that swam soberly through the pond. The owner, as lacking in a sense of humour as his carp, thundered at Little Hugh as he bore down on him.

"I'm not after your fish," protested the youth. "It's

nobody's fish until somebody's catched him."

Later he came to know this to be no defence. It had served as a law in feudal times and perhaps the landlord owed his rights to it, but he sheltered under a new law and Little Hugh was fined, not for the giant carp, fussy of appetite and hard to lure, but for the tasteless perch he had managed to hook, three miserable little fishes with spiky fins.

The fine had to be paid. Hugh fell in with an old man netting a burrow and in a month he had raised the money. The way of a hare he came to know and the way of a pheasant, a partridge, and, of course, the rabbit. He got to know the kind of ferret, the kind of dog to have, and the use of the gate net, long net and whistle and kite. In more than forty years he gathered all the ways of taking game and the ways of disposing of it, too. He was encouraged by an hotel-keeper, and a fish merchant who sold rabbits and an odd brace of birds. He got to know one or two people in the town who liked, and could afford, jugged hare or roast pheasant.

"Pheasant?" he will say. "Me eat pheasant? I never tasted one in my life. Far too fancy for me, is pheasant. No, rabbit's good enough for us."

In this he differs from some of his country neighbours who hold strange beliefs concerning rabbit, which, among other things, they say breeds with rats, being a rodent, is alive with worms, and has "the consumption something awful".

He is well-known in spite of his country knowledge and natural cunning. The pheasants go scarce in what was a good covert and the talk in the public-house

16

mentions Little Hugh as it might mention the fox when chickens are going astray.

"Hugh, boy," someone will say, "they tell me old Gower is losin' birds. Somebody's clearin' the place of them long-tails. He's kept watch, but never seen a thing."

Little Hugh may take a drink before he speaks. His eyes will seem more blue and innocent than ever. "There's all kinds of things after a pheasant," he will say. "There's fox an' stoats an' hawks an' whatnot."

17

THE taking of a hare can be done in three ways, the use of a gun, the use of a snare and the use of a net, and all three need the study of the particular ground. Little Hugh would favour a snare or a net, but Francie McGinn would want to shoot his hare, being a bolder character with more convictions.

The gate net—sometimes it is also used for partridges —is a thing designed for a hare. It is a little bigger in area than a five-barred gate, big enough to drape over the top bar and billow a little below the bottom one. It can only be used with real success after dark. When you want a gate net, learn the knots and make one yourself. I doubt whether you will buy one easily nowadays, and even if the ironmonger has them hanging in hanks you will be wiser to let them hang, for small talk in the ironmonger's shop will take word to the keeper and they will be watching for you after a hare at night, or sneaking up on a covey when dusk has fallen. The night to use the gate net is the night when you can just see the clouds in the sky and yet not have enough moonlight to see the lines in your palm. If it is calm and still, stay at home, for the hare can hear the farm door closing and the bus labouring up the back hill out of the town when you can hear nothing but the beat of your own heart. Take a night when the light is right, for it will help you to escape without falling if you are discovered. If you go when it is as black as the under-stair cupboard, and the keeper comes across you by accident, you will stumble and clatter from here into the next county and probably be caught. There should be a breeze to cover your approach, a sound in the poplar tree like the waves on the shore, a whispering through the wood. Take half a dozen small stones and Little Hugh's dog, until I have told you about dogs and you have trained your own. The stones are to balance along the top of the gate, holding the net up and to keep it to the ground beneath.

19

When the net is in place you will lie a little to the side of the gateway; not too far away, for when the time comes you will have to be there to take the hare. Let your companion go quietly to the far side of the field with the dog and begin his walk. You can hear the thump of his stick and the sound of his boot striking a stone, and the hare you marked this morning can hear it too. He was somewhere in the field when you went quietly round stopping the runs. There is a piece of gorse blocking the hole through the hedge and another at the hole in the drystone wall.

He is moving nervously out there now, bouncing slowly along a draining hollow, uneasy, for he can both hear and smell the dog. They are closer to him. He wheels and goes off across the field, moving fast for the hole in the hedge. Now he has changed direction and is making for the hole in the wall. The dog has the scent of him. The hare has turned again. He is coming down the side of the wall more like a low-flying bird than a running animal. He senses the man and the dog coming across the open field. He swerves in an arc and comes for the gate. It is a silent thing. The net is moving gently in the breeze one minute and the next it is tangled about the hare. All you heard was the small stones falling and the soft scuffle. Be quick. Fall on him. Get him. Strike with the side of your open hand. Chop hard and break his neck. One clean blow and he is dead. Did you see the scurrying shadow? He had a mate. She went under the gate while you were laying him on the bank. Give the curlew whistle softly and get the net rolled, ready for the journey home.

The art of snaring a hare is in making sure that he will not snap the wire. With strong wire fast about his neck he has the power to kick so hard that the strands will snap. Some experts with the snare believe in twisting a thicker strand for a hare, but even set among rushes the snare may be seen. The real way to make sure of him is to set the noose up on its teal or pin, and tie the cord, not to a peg, but to a stone or a draining tile laid well back from the run, and concealed with grass or whatever natural covering is at hand. The hare will run into the noose and, when he kicks, the stone will give and bob a few feet with him. Before it has gone a yard he will be dead and spared the agony of struggle. Sometimes you can set for a hare as you would for a rabbit, but more often than not you will find the wire broken.

Francie McGinn, who cares very little who sees him, and who can walk faster over rough ground than many men over a smooth road, would prefer to shoot a hare. You must study the habits of the hare and note where he sleeps. When the wind is blowing, get down wind so that the sound of your approach will be carried away, and walk him up. Put the dog from you, unless he is trained to your heel, or he may run forward to take the scent on the wind, and when the hare rises you may shoot the dog, as cleverer men have done. These are the ways of coming by a hare. Some may venture after him with a yelping of whippets, but they will oftener see the streaking brownness of him than hold him by the ears.

Finally, make sure you have a market for a hare.

He is not always an easy thing to sell, for the women-folk are not over-eager to prepare him for the pot. Carrying him, as I have said, take a grip of the ears, for this keeps the blood in the stomach so that it can be drained off for the making of soup.

To know the art thoroughly you must study the bread and butter of the professional—the rabbit, and the ways of the rabbit. He is everywhere. Dusk and dawn are his best times. Most of the day, noon and afternoon, when the sun dies and a cold little wind rustles the hedge, he sleeps in his burrow and must be persuaded out with a ferret. Get yourself a ferret, and when you have one you need a marking dog and purse nets, yes, and a short-handled shovel and all the patience of a boy dangling a hook in a pond.

Anton, who lives in a cottage at the tail of the village, will sell you a ferret in June for ten shillings. Anton is a mole-catcher and, among other things, he breeds ferrets. There are two kinds of ferret, the little lemon beast and the brown and yellow polecat. If Little Hugh comes with us to Anton's you will finish with two ferrets; a little one because he is agile, and a polecat because he has the power to shift a full-grown old buck who might sit tight in the burrow and fight with the kicks of his back legs. Little Hugh had better come, for Anton can see you know nothing about ferrets at a glance. If you go alone he will sell you a ferret for ten shillings, then offer to train him for you for five shillings more, saying, "Come back in a month." On your return he will take the five shillings and a further shilling as the cost of the ferret's keep, and all the training your ferret will have had will be the run round the inside of a barrel when Anton cleaned the boxes!

The cost will include Anton's advice on the care of ferrets.

"Don't overfeed him. Keep him dry and watch out for the distemper. Ten shillings, please, an' lucky you are to be gettin' him at the price, for in October the price would be a pound. Feed him raw meat. Set some mousetraps for birds."

I can't recommend Anton to you. He is a cruel brute. He can never be bothered to put a muzzle on a ferret, he will tell you. It is far easier to take a darning needle and tack the lips together, letting the poor creature run the burrows this way, often ravenously hungry. Give him his price and let us get away. The stench is not only the smell of his ferret boxes.

Take the advice of Little Hugh and make a pet of the ferret. Feed it well, but no better than you would a dog, for it will get fat and unhealthy. Get into the way of carrying him in your pocket, but be very careful he doesn't wriggle out. He is slippery as an eel and will often find a small hole in a sack that is tied at the neck. There is only one way of becoming friendly with the little hunter—handle him often. When you reach for him, calm your nerves. Let the motion of your hand be steady and deliberate or you will find him as firmly fixed to your fingers as he might fix himself to the throat of his quarry, for he is nervous and excitable.

There are burrows in the woodside and some of them are linked with others from here to the village. Among these tunnels are the roots of trees and old tough fibres, dank and crumbling little-used paths, twisting and winding in a maze. This is no place to put down the new ferret. Go along the hedge and let him have a trial at the little warren with a dozen holes. You can put on a muzzle to stop him killing and lying up, or let him run loose. I like to let him run loose, for if the keeper comes and he has to be abandoned, he can survive. Some poachers use a line and collar, by which means they can drag the poor little beast back, although oftener than not he has carried the line in a double loop round the roots of the hedge and the pulling only ties him in his grave.

Hold him above the shoulders and put him down. He goes into the hole sniffing and showing interest. Stand back and say nothing. Watch the nets. It may be ten or fifteen minutes if he goes methodically through the warren, or he may show again in a few seconds. Put him back, for he has only worked a few yards. Hold your breath and take a look through the hedge in case the keeper is coming. Is every hole netted carefully?

The clock in the church tower chimed a while ago and now it strikes the half-hour. When did he come up last? He showed at a hole-mouth for an instant. Was it near the gorse or up the bank? Perhaps he is blocked somewhere or he has killed and is lying up to eat, after which he will doze for the rest of the day. Lie down and put an ear to the ground. A sound of thumping? An old long-toothed buck defending himself? Steady. It seemed to come from over there. It is moving. Like a ball from a cannon the rabbit is up and the net is about him like an old woman's string-bag. Hurry and lift him. Break his neck as you did that of the hare and set the net once more. The ferret is out through the mesh. He seems to blink in the strong light of day, as though he had been down to the devil and back. Put him in again. He hurries back, wondering perhaps how the buck slipped past him down there.

26

Now he has startled the doe and she is sitting behind a net, petrified because he is creeping through the burrow with his musky odour drifting before him. Get her. Under the blackthorn there is an old hole clogged with leaves and we have missed it. That rustle was another escaping, crossing the bank and racing out over the field on the other side of the hedge. It is time to lift nets and put the ferret back in your pocket. Dusk seems to be crawling out of the wood and across the misty fields.

The nets you take ferreting will be new and white. Get a handful of soil and rub it into the cord so that it turns brown, otherwise the rabbit may see them and turn back, making the job longer. If you stand too close you will certainly frighten him, so stand away and leave it to the ferret. Keep the gun at hand, so that if the rabbit slips the net you can tumble him before he gets far.

Ferrets have a habit of blocking just about dusk. The afternoon is wearing away and you can hear the owl. It is colder and the excitement is waning. When that moment arrives and the ferret is below ground, look at your watch. As sure as you heard a cock pheasant call in the copse he will stay down and you have lost him. There are things called "stinkers" for getting a ferret back; a kind of charm in their way. Block most of the holes and light a "stinker" in one that is left unblocked. It should smoulder and in time drive out your ferret. It is sometimes a slow process. Little Hugh prefers a lump of gorse. He pushes the gorse in a hole-mouth and lights it, making sure he has the wind behind him. In a short time, when the wind has carried the smoke through the burrow, the ferret will evacuate. I have known rabbits caught in this way on a windy day. If you do not starve the ferret to make him fierce, a practice as savage as the old country method of slitting a jackdaw's tongue to make it talk, he is not so likely to stay below, but if he does, there are one or two ways that may move him if he is near the entrance to a burrow. Take the rabbit caught earlier and push it into the hole, slowly withdrawing it again and repeating the performance. The scent and movement will bring him unless he has killed. If you have no rabbit, take a blade of grass between the thumbs and blow against it so that it makes a squealing noise. A ferret has the curiosity of his brother, the stoat, and will respond to the sound as he would to the squeals of a dying rabbit. He will even chase a twig if it is pushed into a hole and moved provocatively and he will come out after it like an angry kitten.

However, no matter how fortunate you are in most things, the day will arrive when the ferret stays down. You will burn your "stinker" and gorse, use the lure, thump, squeak and coax without result. The average poacher takes a good look round, lies down and listens carefully and then takes up his shovel or whin-hoe and starts the process of digging. Burrows extend according to the nature of the ground. On a well-drained slope, where the soil is light, the warren may be a network covering fifty or a hundred yards. The network may be eighteen inches below the surface or three feet down, going deeper through the roots of a tree. The digging will raise perspiration and mounds of earth. Every now and then it will be necessary to take another look for the coming of the keeper or the farmer.

In the company of two Welsh poachers I once spent a whole afternoon digging up a bank. We cursed the ferret in the common tongue and I grunted my approval of the equivalents in Welsh. Just at dark, when we were agreed that he had gone as deep as we had wished him, we saw a glint of something white on the stubble. It was our ferret. Tiring of the noise perhaps, he had quietly sneaked out and was on his way across the field, running springily in the half light. We threw down our tools and made after him, but he skipped in the air and disappeared into a hole by a partly uprooted stump. It was too dark to do any more. We staggered back and fumbled for our nets and made our way home.

Usually when a ferret goes down and cannot be dug out the poacher makes a despairing effort to block every hole with a stone, hoping to keep the ferret below ground over-night so that he is eager to come out when the holes are opened in daylight. Ferrets lie up when they have gorged themselves and seem as comfortable in the stuffiness of the burrow as a rabbit which stays down through a day-long rainstorm. Put down a lined ferret, some poachers say, and the lined ferret, scenting the blood of the kill, will lie up with his mate; then all you have to do is to dig along the line. This process may mean altering the entire landscape, moving rocks and trees and going deeper than the brock, who loves the bowels of the earth.

The dog that marked for us. Francie McGinn is the man for a dog. He can make friends with the fiercest dog and train anything with four legs and a tail. I

walked behind Francie once. We were walking up a
lane that passed through a farmyard. Francie did
not know I was behind. As he reached the gate into
the yard he gave his cur a signal. I dawdled, letting an
elderbush screen me. Francie went on. The dog
bounded up over a stone wall and went noiselessly
through a rickyard. I reached the gate and went
through. Ahead of me Francie slouched with his
hands in his waist-pockets and a piece of sweet grass
in his teeth. There was no sound, but, like a shadow,
his dog came squeezing under a gate. Francie bent
down and took the chicken from its mouth. In a
moment he had the fowl in the lining of his jacket and
was patting the dog when I reached him.

"A clever dog you have there," I said.

"Infernal clever," he agreed.

He did not say a word about the chicken. A feather

tumbled from under his jacket. He shook his lapel and another fell to the dust.

"Infernal clever," he said again, chewing on the grass. "I've sold him twice, an' would you believe it, he come back the very next day both times!"

I wondered about the purchase money. Francie's money burned his pocket until he had a pint-pot in his hand.

The dog should be no bigger than a terrier and have courage and cunning. It should mark and hunt without barking. In the bar, just before closing time, when the imagination is stimulated and they are telling those stories of two-headed calves and the strange ways of rats stealing eggs, they will give you information on the ways of stopping a dog barking. Thrash him until he can hardly walk; put tobacco plug down the poor creature's throat; cut the end off his tongue. These are the men who will sew a ferret's lips or break off his fangs with a pair of pincers. It is a strange fact that these cruel theories persist even among men who are otherwise gentle and humane, considerate of the horses they tend, patient with the sickly lamb. Do none of these things. Pick a steady pup. Be firm but gentle and introduce it to hunting carefully. Let it get over its excitement and reward it when it responds. It must have a good nose. Two poachers will meet and stand for a long time looking at dogs, making proud claims for "the nose" of their particular dog and its stout-hearted entry through gorse and blackthorn after an escaping rabbit. Your dog must have a strong constitution and, above all, must go home at an order when you run into trouble.

Once I borrowed a dog. His owner met me as I left for the woods and, seeing I had no dog with me, persuaded me to go to his cottage and ask his wife to let me have the dog. It turned out to be an old terrier of sorts, dim of eye and both slow and waddling in his gait. I could not refuse. The poacher's family stood about me assuring me in chorus that Spider would get me rabbits. We departed for the bracken and gorse slope. When I reached the end of the patch the old terrier was still fussing round a few sticks of dead bracken. I called to him but he remained there. I added deafness to my mental list of his infirmities, called again and then walked on. The dog did not come. I was out of gunshot when the pheasant rose from before his nose. He stood and looked at me in disgust. I took him home, stepped over the children playing at the door, and expressed my thanks and hoped that the old dog could not talk.

The pheasant can hear to-night's thunderstorm coming; the rabbit and hare can both hear and feel the vibration of your approach. The dog with a nose scents the partridge in the strong tang of the swede field, the rabbit in the heavy perfume of the gorse, the hare lying in the clover and the pheasant in the lower branches of the fir tree.

With a good dog you can go after rabbits with a gun, with purse nets or a long net. I have seen a man taking rabbits with only a dog and purse nets. On an autumn day, lured across the fields by the sight of a pheasant on a strip of new ploughing, I came upon a man and a dog in a hollow. They did not see me, for when I move I go quietly, keeping off the bare skyline and in the shadow as much as I can. He was a gipsy and his dog was a skin-and-bone whippet. When the dog marked a blackberry bush the man took purse nets out of his pocket and crept quietly round the clump draping nets over every exit. When he had done he began to bombard the bush with stones. A rabbit bolted and became entangled in one of the nets. Before it could struggle free the lean, long-legged gipsy was there, with his whippet keeping an alert watch behind him as he seized the rabbit and broke its neck. While I watched he caught four, and afterwards, when we met on the road, he offered to sell them to me at a ridiculous price, because, I imagine, I was wearing a new-looking coat and was therefore wealthy enough.

To go after rabbits with the long net you need company. A long net cannot be managed alone. It has to be rolled out and set up with sticks, and for this help is needed. In the choice of companions you must be careful. You may talk for a long time in a village before being on terms with poachers that will enable you to arrange an expedition. The fraternity are cautious. They will exchange views about places worth trying and the means of going about it, but it will be no more than talk. They know you are inexperienced, or that you made a fool of yourself by taking to your heels before old Wilson's ploughman when he met you after a hare.

Not long ago a friend who came by a long net—he moved into a cottage and discovered it in an out-house—talked two acquaintances into a night's work. They darned the holes in the net as well as they knew how, borrowed a dog and went to the public-house for a drink or two to give them heart, leaving the net, of course, behind a hedge in case the keeper happened to be taking heart in the same bar. When the place closed they staggered down the road and made their way across the fields to the woodside like a stampede of cart-horses. Two of them took fright at the threatening shadow of a small thorn tree and the third tripped and let the dog go free, whereupon the animal made for home in a streak of frantically working legs. The three poachers set up the net, struggling to unravel tangles and searching with matches for sticks that had dropped. One had to play the part of the dog, and when the net was up, off he went round the field giving out excited yelps that startled a flock of sheep. In ten minutes the feet of the sheep had dragged the net away from its pins, broken it and tangled it in such a manner that it was quite useless. The two who waited for the kill had retreated to the hedge, where they sat at the bottom of an ash tree and fell soundly asleep. In the grey light, walking home with the broken net, they were overtaken by a policeman, who took them in charge.

Be patient. Get to know the community. When you have gone once or twice with the ferret someone may suggest a night with the long net. More likely you will be asked to come just to stand by and listen, or keep a look-out if there is enough of a moon.

On my first expedition with the long net I was helper to Francie. He is a bold character. A long time ago he was chased by a keeper who fired a shot at him. The pellets of lead entered Francie's neck.

They did no more than raise a few beads of blood. Some were hooked out by Francie's mother with a darning needle. The others remained. Francie is quite proud of them and he will ask you to feel them as they roll under his skin at the pressure of your finger, saying, "Number four shot, them. Enough there to bring down a goose!" On another occasion, running at full speed down a ride in a wood, he tripped over a stretched wire and sprawled on his face. A second wire, set close to the first, cut him across the bridge of his nose. The injury so infuriated Francie that he waited for his pursuer and laid him low with the butt of his gun.

Francie and I took stable lanterns. A lighted lantern shows for miles, but we were on the secluded side of a wood and in the shelter of a hill. These lanterns were Francie's bravado. It is safer to work with a flash-lamp or a small lamp of some kind, for the storm lantern shows for miles when it has to be carried along the net so that the rabbits are dazzled and can be lifted quickly. I knew Frància hoped for some kind of excitement. We had three dozen rabbits at the first setting and had them in a sack and the net rolled, ready for moving on, when we heard a stone fall from a dyke. Francie stood out from the shelter of the wood, his outline a dark patch on the grey of the field.

"Haste you down the woodside an' away," he whispered.

Groaning under my burden, I staggered off with the sack, the net and the sticks. Behind me Francie stood like a post in the field. Once I was safely on the road I put the net and the sack in the ditch and sat down to wait. Francie joined me in half an hour. He had walked round the keeper twice, he said, and had half thought of lighting the lantern I had left behind. I was thankful to get home that night.

An outing with Francie has excitement and real danger. He is the kind of man who prefers a bold march across an estate to skulking in the hedges. As he goes he watches for movement with the corner of his eye, quick to notice a figure making a line from a· farmyard. Shoot and move on is his motto. Never stand where you have shot something, he will tell you, but get away out of it as quickly as possible. Yet he is not without cunning and he certainly has humour, for once he made boldly to a copse, where the keeper had been feeding pheasants, carrying a yard broom under his arm like a gun and a sack slung over his shoulder. On the way back he was pounced upon by the keeper and calmly gave up the sack of leaves he had swept up in the copse! A wild character if ever

I kept one company, Francie is the kind of man who will insist on stopping to hold off pursuit while his companions get away. He has been in prison several times and is always penitent before the law.

"Bad company. I'm sorry," he said once. "Treat me fair an' I'll not be up again, I promise you. I wouldn't ha' been up now but for pure hard luck!"

The setting of a long net is a thing no aspiring poacher can master without the instruction of a man who has actually put down a net and succeeded in catching rabbits by this means. A long net may be seventy-five yards, but more often it is a hundred yards in length, and three feet or so in width. Threaded through the net are two cords, one at the top and the other at the bottom. At either end are steel pins which are driven into the ground and the net is supported by sticks a little over three feet long.

To run out a net requires skill. It must have been lifted in the right way on the last expedition or it will come out in tangles and half the night will be spent in putting it right. As a rule the first steel pin is driven into the ground by one of the setters while the man with the net retreats a pace, letting the first hank out of the great bag he wears round his neck. With the first hank comes the first wooden peg or stick. The net is drawn to the ground after the stick has been set up and the bottom cord is looped firmly round the stick. The second hank comes out; the net stretches twelve feet or so between each peg and the process of looping the cords and pushing the pegs into the ground continues until the full length has been set in a straight line. It is all done in absolute silence.

37

When the whole of the net stands pegged a final tightening and adjusting takes place, and then the dog, or one of the poachers, goes round the field to drive the rabbits in, and cover all the ground before the net. The dog must be one trained not to rush in after the rabbits or chaos will result!

As the rabbits strike the net the meshes bag up and hold him. There is enough slack to bag all the rabbits. The cords hold fast and the mesh is too small—about two inches square—to allow the rabbit to bolt through. One of the secrets is in knowing where to set and another in setting so that the wind billows the net away from the running rabbit.

One experience long ago taught me that a gin is a brutal means of catching a rabbit. I had been searching through what used to be our cheese loft and came across a tin trunk containing a dozen old iron traps. They were the vicious-looking spring-handled type with serrated jaws and tethering chains strong enough to hold a sheep. Anton, on one of his mole-catching visits, had carried a few in his bag and had shown me how to set them by standing on the handle and carefully juggling the platform and tongue over one of the jaws. Without much thought I gathered them and put them in a sack, and the following morning, for it was late afternoon when I found them, I carried the sack to a distant hill.

There were holes in the hillside, but I preferred to set them in the runs through the stone wall. Down in the corner of the field there was a particularly well-worn path beneath a slab of stone. I had visions of a hare or at least a rabbit every day. I struggled manfully but found only one of the traps responding, because of rust. This trap I thrust into the hole in the wall, covering the platform with a few straws of dead grass, and proceeded to stamp the tethering peg firmly into the ground.

Next morning I arrived and got down on my hands and knees to peer into the hole before pulling out the gin. A hedgehog had been killed between the jaws. I released the body and reset the trap. The next morning I found another and on the third morning, becoming careless, I thrust my hand into the hole before looking, and the gin, which had been empty, clamped firmly to my wrist! The teeth, as sharp as those of a farm dog, buried themselves in my flesh. In agony I withdrew my hand and the gin came scraping and jingling with it. I had not the strength to remove it by depressing the spring with my hands, for even a grown man must stand on it to release the jaws. I set to work on the tethering pin, so well fixed in the stony ground. The peg, too, was immovable. After ten minutes I gave up and through my tears contemplated the trap on my arm. Little trickles of blood from the cuts ran down to my finger tips and splashed on my knees. I had an awful vision of myself starving to death, tethered in the corner by the wall like a goat, and screened by some of the tallest gorse for miles. In imagination I lay at dusk, weak and with the mist forming beads of moisture on the wool of my jersey, listening to the bark of the collie at home at milking time, shivering at the ghostly moan of the wind through the stones.

I was not just sorry for myself. I was more frightened

D

than I had ever been before. When I recovered my composure I set my teeth and began the painful process of moving my wrist in the gin. Every small movement brought fresh tears. As the teeth of the gin dragged over my flesh the skin was ploughed up. Several times I had to stop and close my eyes until, finally, with the last rally of my courage, I held the gin in my free hand and ripped my other hand from its grip. The sight of my wrist, bleeding and swollen, frightened me so that I could not look at it again for a while. I stood up and made my way through the gorse, leaving the trap, where it may lie to this day for all I know. I never set another, and once shot a fox I found tied down by one in the heart of a wood.

The snare, properly set, is one of the cleanest and most humane ways of killing a rabbit. Snaring has little excitement. It is a thing a man does on a quiet afternoon when there may be a bit of a drizzle or a mist, wandering over rough ground where there are no sheep to become noosed by the feet. An old ewe can snap a snare with a couple of kicks, but in that time it may bite deeply into her slender leg and almost cut her foot off. Rough ground, dotted with gorse and patches of round rushes, is the best snaring place. You will find it criss-crossed with runs. On its way to feed, a rabbit will make deviations something like a hare, which seems to have a peculiar course, zigzagging and traversing from one side of the field to the other, first along the hollow of a sunken drain and then tacking back over a path all its own, like a ship sailing up-wind. An expert with a snare looks at a run and knows just where to set. He sees in the faint signs of flattened and standing grass just where the rabbit is on the jump and where he lands. He will set past the jump and the pear-shaped noose will be four fingers' width from the ground. This has to be judged, because a run will hold the scent of a man's hand.

The snare must not be too near the first setting, for if one or the other catches, the struggles may frighten a rabbit on the adjoining run. A buck bounds into the noose and is dead in a minute, but a doe may squeal and her squeals attract a weasel or stoat, or even

a poaching dog. The countryman has a way of protecting his catch. To the twine of the snare he will tie two or three small tins. When the rabbit struggles the tins clatter and scare away the stoat, which will only fix on a live prey. There is another way of protecting the snared rabbit, a way as old as hunting. A hazel rod is driven into the ground and bowed down over the run. To the end of the rod a short piece of cord is tied, and this cord is also fastened to a notched peg as well as the cord of the snare. The notched peg is engaged in a notch in a pin in the ground. When the rabbit is in the snare its first movement frees the notched peg and allows the hazel rod to whip upright, carrying the snared rabbit up out of harm's way, where it hangs until the setter returns.

Once I saw a buck and doe running close together and, coming to a snare, both were noosed. Often rabbits run and brush snares aside because they were badly set or set at the wrong height. Little Hugh, an expert in all the methods of rabbit-catching, is fond of setting a snare in a wire fence. He sets at the point where the rabbit goes over or under the lowest strand and dangles a noose from a tethering pin twined in the higher strands of the fence. In this way he has more than once caught not only rabbits but an odd cock pheasant.

There is perhaps no more risky way of poaching than by snaring. The beginner would do well to set no more than a dozen. It is not so simple as it seems. The runs may be fresh or they may be little used. The snare-setter has to know the rabbit and hare run from the path of the sheep, the run of the badger and the fox, or he will come to find his snare drawn out, snapped or swept aside by a lumbering beast twice as high as the rabbit. Every snare must be weathered. It is foolish to set snares that are freshly cut and whittled. After the tethering and setting pins are cut they should be buried in soil until they become stained. If they are simply rubbed with earth they will wash white in a night-shower. The best pins are to be had in a hazel thicket. Cut them and carry them away before trimming the points and slitting the tips to hold the noose. The gamekeeper may stand in the wood looking at your pile of chips and deducing that someone is getting ready for a season with the snares.

Before looking for snares it is as well to explore the field carefully. The gamekeeper has a habit of lying about waiting for a poacher to come and lift his snares. He will even go so far as to bait one if there has been no catch, simply to be able to capture the offender "with a coney in his possession" as they say in court. There is nothing to do but to study the cover, look at the thorn tree, the patch of elderberry in the hollow, the mounds of gorse and the sheltering wall. Walk through casually and ignore the snares. Most gamekeepers are as fond of bed in the early morning as anyone else. Rabbits run at nightfall and at daybreak. It is useless to go before dawn. Better wait until the smoke is showing on the chimneys of the village and the milk lorry is crashing on its way along the back road to pick up churns from road-end platforms.

Remember to lay no more than you can lift, for you may have too many to reset and a heavy burden to carry. While you are stooping to adjust a pin the keeper may be coming with running strides from the hedge, his dogs bustling about him as he bears down upon you. As you make your escape you may have the misfortune to fall with your foot in one of your own snares, as Little Hugh once did. It is a business calling for wits. You must be more alive than the trio that crawled through the wood last night after roosting pheasants.

The cottager is fonder of snaring than any other way

of poaching. He can slip from his back door and put down three or four without much chance of being seen. Isolated, he can take his time before going to look and need not worry about the gossip of his neighbours. If the stoat has been there before him he is happier, because he is less fastidious than the townsman. The rabbit he snares is for his own dinner, and the stoat only draws off the warm blood, leaving the flesh of the rabbit as white as chicken. Even the foraging magpie will take no more than the eyes. The dealer, however, will have no stoat-drained rabbits. A poacher selling his catch has many problems. If he sells to individuals he becomes too well advertised for the good of his business. If he sells to a dealer he may be betrayed to the keeper or the police if he refuses the price he is offered.

The rabbit, I have said, is the bread and butter of the poacher. Probably the rabbit has been the cause of more poachers going to prison and being fined than any other animal or bird. The poaching of rabbits gets in the blood of hundreds of country boys. The ragged youngster at the village school tries his hand at it as surely as he sets a line for the trout or goes gathering plover eggs on a Sunday in April. The farmer's son is certain to do it more than once and even the parson's son falls to the temptation.

In the village on Saturday I often see the poachers leaving. They are home from work in a hurry, gulp down a dinner and whistle for their dogs. There is nonchalance about them and you might not spot them. One wears an old raincoat and an earth-stained battledress. He has a knapsack under his raincoat and only the handle of his shovel shows from the sack he is carrying. He might be going to work in a garden but for the dog running ahead and a certain look of excitement and determination on his face. Another wears a coat tied at the waist with twine. The bulges are nets in one pocket and ferret in the other. It will be dark before they return and they may sell a rabbit in the "Sun" to-night for the price of two jugs of ale. Twenty years ago values were much the same!

You may net and snare rabbits, but for enjoyment the way to get them is to beat through gorse with a gun. Pick a back hill and a windy day, so that the sound of your shot will be carried away like the bird

flying with the gale. Go in through the blackthorn across the marshy patch and on up to the edge of the wood. When you have shot twice, move on. Make for good cover and stand for a long time listening. You will hear all manner of little sounds, the timid chirp of the wren, the drumming of the woodpecker and the sound of leaves drifting down to make a carpet on the ground. Listen to the distant cockcrow, the tractor buzzing in the field, the lowing of the cow, and distinguish from all these the sound of the game-

45

keeper's boot on the board of the stile, a heelshod against a stone, a cracking twig. Without a sound the small birds will come over, frightened by the keeper's progress along the path through the trees, a pigeon will burst from the top of a near-by fir and it is time for you to go, to go noiselessly as the fox skirts the place where a man is. The keeper has ways of knowing you have been in the wood. He will pick up your bright red cartridge case, noting whether it is weathered or not, and the bore, too. When you have fired unload the case into your palm and put it in your pocket, especially if you are using a poacher's gun, the folding four-ten, or one with a smaller bore than a twelve, perhaps a sixteen or a twenty.

One of the poachers in the village where I live has the habit of picking a time to go with his gun when no other human would venture. There comes a raw storm of hail, peppering furrows of autumn ploughing and beating the last leaves off the trees, or a downpour so heavy that it travels across the fields like sheets of glass, and this man puts a scarf round his head, buttons a greatcoat about him and makes for the wood and the comparative shelter of the trees, turning his back against the gale like a horse, bowing a little as the sheep seem to do. In the wood he may disturb a pheasant moving daintily to drier cover, or a pigeon may come drifting in on the sweep of the wind. Whatever he disturbs, he will not move the neatly trimmed hazel rods the keeper leaves about so that he may know, if they have been taken, that someone has been in the wood. There is a considerable advantage in picking such a time.

46

47

BLACK BILL was already an old man when I was a child. I remember meeting him, or passing him at any rate, when I was being walked home from the "preaching" at the country school-house one Sunday evening in early summer. My aunts had a firm belief that a preaching was a good thing for a small boy, if it only taught him to sit still and keep quiet for an hour and a half, and how hard it was to seem attentive to the preacher when, behind the school-house the pigeons called through the wood, and close by its door ran a singing stream!

"Here's that character, Black Bill!" one whispered to the other as they hurried me along.

"He's a bit like Jesus," I said solemnly as I took note of that character, and indeed he might well have been an apostle, for he had large soulful eyes and a curly black beard.

"Think shame!" my aunts scolded in unison and averted their gaze while we passed Black Bill.

I looked at him and he smiled; then all at once I lost his attention, for he switched his regard to a green finch that flew up and seemed to throw itself over the hedge. My boots squeaked as I plodded homeward. After a while I turned my head and looked back. Black Bill was hanging about a watering hole at the side of the road and probably observing a waterhen I had noticed there as we had hurried past.

"Well," I said quietly to assuage the shocked religious feelings of my elders, "if he's not like Jesus he's a bit like John the Baptist!"

"He's a good-for-nothing old poacher!" said one of them.

"He's a dirty old tramp!" added the other, "and he catches little goldfinches and sells them, and The Lord will punish him!"

"He looked like The Lord to me," I said.

For the rest of the journey home through the gathering dusk, under the ash trees, through the floating clouds of midges and up the footpath and over the stile until we came to the whitewashed farm with its peat smoke going up to the night, I heard the history of Black Bill, disciple of the devil, so they said.

Black Bill was a man for birds, they told me. He just naturally went after any kind of bird; the bantams of Willie Adair, the fowls of the schoolmistress, the guinea birds of Mrs. McQuade, the little bird that sang in the tree and, worst of all, the pheasants and partridges in every wood and field for miles and miles.

49

"He's an ill character," they wound up as we reached the farm kitchen, "the like of which we wouldn't have about the place. Your grandmother once lost a setting of turkey eggs through Black Bill, the villain! Your grandfather encouraged him here, to spite the gamekeeper for something they had fallen out about, but he was glad to see the back of him, we can tell you!"

My grandfather had been dozing by the fire. He sat up and lit his pipe, running a spill quickly through his fingers to quench its flame as he always did.

"Black Bill?" he said. "Black Bill can charm a bird off a tree. He has the way of such things. He keeps a whistle in his pocket and, when he's near a bird, he plays a bit of a tune, I've heard."

"He sounds a gentle man," I ventured.

My grandfather laughed.

"A black-hearted, wild savage!" said one of my aunts coming from down the hall, where she had been to hang her coat.

It was a long time before I got to know the truth of Black Bill, the man who could charm the little bird. I did not see him again for ten years or more. By that time I had taken to mooching the hedges with an old gun and had had the lessons of Francie and Little Hugh to add to those of Jeck.

There is a time, just after harvest, when the ground seems shorn, yet green with exposed clover; when the hare is uncovered and runs in the sight of man and the partridge coveys are scattered more often. On autumn days, before the first cold wind comes, the poacher begins to take note of the movement of the partridges, listens to the "two-thri" call they make at nightfall and thinks about the net and the gun. I had been walking through a field of roots, hoping to put up partridges, and came to the hedge above the road. My heart bounded when I suddenly knew I was being watched, and then relief came when I realised that the watcher was not my enemy, the keeper. I looked at Black Bill. He stood in a gateway, his hands thrust deeply into the pockets of his over-large jacket, his black head and beard a tousled tangle. I went to the gate and bade him good afternoon.

"I was looking for a partridge," I said.

"A partridge?" He fumbled in his pocket and brought out a brass whistle made from the ends of two cartridges.

"Two-thri, two-thri, two-thri," he whistled.

It was the call of the partridge collecting the covey, rasping, pausing and beginning again; the sound that was somehow dusk and the pathetic bleating of sheep when the last glow of the sun had gone off the highest hill. Black Bill's lips parted and showed remarkably white teeth while he whistled. Now he turned and swung his arm up, quietly pointing over the field. I caught my breath. Out of the ragged furrows of turnips a partridge ventured, inquisitive; a foot raised and held up, then delicately put down on the dusty earth; a movement through the motionless leaves and the straggling sorrel and another of the covey followed the first. They stood near each other, necks a little stretched, immaculate and beautiful little brown birds. I could only watch. I was no longer the poacher after a partridge. Black Bill looked at me. I shook my head silently. He put his hand to his mouth and removed the whistle from his teeth. The two partridges stood there. I could have killed them, but I could only think of what I had heard of Black Bill, who could lure the birds.

"Shoot them," he said softly.

"A black-hearted savage," I heard my aunt say.

"I couldn't," I said and my voice frightened the birds, for they ran quickly up the furrow as soon as I spoke.

"I couldn't kill a partridge either," said Black Bill. "I could have shot hundreds in my time, thousands, yes!"

"I couldn't shoot them when they come like that," I said, for I had my conscience and I had shot and eaten my share.

"A partridge to some," said Black Bill, "is just a little snack on a plate with gravy runnin' round it."

"I've heard you're a bird-catcher," I said.

He grinned through his whiskers. "The partridge is the one bird I don't touch," he said; "but the old pheasant—now there's a proud an' impudent bird. I never spared one yet!"

We walked along the road together and he let me see his whistle. It was no more than an ordinary cartridge-case whistle, the kind of thing a poacher makes for his son to pass the time in the evening, and takes from him again in a day or two because the incessant noise is driving the family insane! I tried it with poor results. Black Bill explained that it wanted a great deal of practice. As we walked, the cry of a partridge came to us across a dun field of raked stubble. He put the whistle in his mouth and began to make the notes. It needed sharp eyesight to see the covey gathering. We stood a long time while the countryside fell asleep. The partridges came across the stubble, nearer and nearer to us, then Black Bill suddenly clapped his hands and they sank into the cover of the stalks.

They were clustered together, blending with the fawn and brown of the field, as motionless as they would have been had a kestrel hovered above them. I could have walked out and frightened them into flight but it seemed wrong. I followed Black Bill down the road.

Some time after this encounter with Black Bill I made myself a whistle and practised the "two-thri" call. I was using the whistle to no obvious effect when Black Bill came out of a thicket where he had been setting up a trap-cage for a goldfinch.

"Wrong time an' the wrong day for that," he said.

It was a damp day. A mist hung over the hollows. The rape and swedes were wet with rain that had fallen in the night. On such a day partridges keep to the ground and cry little if at all, and even at dusk, when a cold breeze hastens over the hill as though chasing the departing day, they are silent. Such a day is one for walking the furrows with a gun.

On a bright day the partridges are out on the open stubble. Towards night, when there is a frost, they will be closer to the hedge, and even up among the gorse. An odd little call or two, somehow like two stones being scraped together, will rally the covey. In the bright autumn sun of the morning, Black Bill

53

told me, the way to make sure partridges would not fly was to put up a kite, having marked where the covey was feeding. This is a job for two. One man flies the kite, and, incidentally, advertises the thing to every sharp-eyed countryman for miles, while the other gets ready to walk to them with his gun. The partridges, at the first sight of the kite, freeze to the ground as they would for a hawk or falcon. They will then only rise when the poacher walks in among them and puts them to flight. It might seem a cruel deception, but not nearly so cruel as the method of Anton, who, having seen a covey in a turnip field, runs for his traps and sets one in every furrow, after which he beats down the rows with a stick and a tin tray. The birds, running ahead, stand little chance of avoiding the gin and are caught in the biting jaws that crush their little bodies.

54

On the wing partridges are fast. They rise in a
flurry and are gone almost before the unwary man
has time to cock his gun. They go whirring away
down over the field, swinging to the curve of the
ground and planing down out of sight. Hasten to that
very spot where you saw them land and it is most
unlikely you will find one of them, for as soon as they
are on the ground they run.

To hunt partridges you need Little Hugh's dog.
These little birds have a strong scent about them. A
good dog can mark them with no difficulty and, when
he has marked, just consider the lie of the land. Ahead
is a low hedge and to the left a line of trees. On the
right a hazel copse, and behind, a long slope to a wood.
When they burst up from the ground, as though from
the muzzle of a gun, they will speed for the hedge and
skim just over the top, dropping out of sight the
instant they are over. They have not settled but are
flying on a foot or so from the field, or they will turn
back in a great arc and shoot themselves forward down
the slope. At the moment you think they will alight
in the field, they will plane in through the trees, or
even turn and seem to vanish against the background
of brown soil, dead bracken and the tufts of straw
round the potato clamp.

The coveys of the quiet hills are even wilder than
those of the lowlands. They rise quickly and speed
off on the wind. They fly so far and so fast that you
lose sight of them. You plod relentlessly on in the
line of their flight and when you are exhausted they
rise below you and throw themselves over a shoulder
of the hill. The shot you fired echoes across the valley

and you are disturbed to see the figure hastening up the footpath with two spaniels loping ahead. It is time to get out over the skyline and take the shelter of the march wall as fast as your gasping breath will allow. Away below, in the stony field where the hill farmer grew his potatoes, the call is sounding faintly as the wild covey gathers itself once more.

Remember that the partridge, like the pheasant, has a strong game smell. An acquaintance of mine who loved poaching carried his gun with him on his day's work at the plough. Turning over the old harvest field he drew near a covey and got ready. When he was near enough, he put them up and shot one with each barrel. At that moment he heard the keeper shooting two fields away and hurried to hide his kill. It seemed safe enough to raise the furrow and lay them under, hiding his gun in the same place and leaving a small white stone to mark the spot. This he did long before the keeper arrived, and he had, in fact, turned a second furrow beside the first before the keeper was in the field. Keepers, when they are not sure of themselves, affect a deceiving friendliness. They pass the time of day and ask casually, did you hear a shot? Or have you seen anything of one of the notorious poachers? Perhaps you would like a rabbit for dinner? Careful! He waits to hear you say you can't face rabbit any more.

The man at the plough nodded his greeting and limped on a yard or two to the end of the furrow. As the horses stamped and jingled round the keeper put his question. A shot? No. He hadn't noticed. The coulter glided into the soft ground and set up a new steaming paring of earth. The ploughman looked anxiously ahead, ploughing as though taking part in a match. Between the nodding heads of his team he could see the keen-scented spaniels doubling and turning on a scent, padding out over the furrows and returning; taking the message from the breeze, moving nearer to the buried game. The keeper's sharp glance turned from the dogs to the man at the plough, then he looked to the hedge for a hiding place for a gun.

"A hare!" shouted the ploughman.

A hare had risen close to the feet of the horses. At that moment the foremost spaniel had set his feet to the furrow where the partridges were buried. The keeper threw up his gun and the hare tumbled, then recovered and raced under the second shot. The keeper's whistle blew. The wounded hare tumbled again and yet ran on. The two spaniels, called off the furrows, galloped off on the hare's scent. The keeper lumbered after them, reloading his gun with one movement of a hand that carried two cartridges to the breech. The ploughman halted his horses and stood to watch. The man and his dogs disappeared through the next field. In ten minutes another shot sounded. In that time the partridges were out of the furrow and in the breast of the ploughman's shirt and the gun safely laid in a fresh furrow. The keeper and his dogs returned. The spaniels cast about, took the old scent and dug in the furrow. The keeper scratched his head and blew his whistle again and the ploughman smiled at the ears of his horses.

The partridge makes her nest in the low blackberry bush at the edge of the field, among the dwarfed gorse, in the tall grass that will soon know the reaper. The brood run almost as soon as they are hatched, like all birds of the ground. The mother protects them from man and beast by appearing to have a broken wing. by seeming unable to fly and fluttering a yard or two and coming to earth, agitated and somehow bewildered. The unwary human hastens after her, two, three, four strides, and then she rises and flutters from him so that he hurries again to catch her. When he is lured away from the youngsters she will rise and fly out over the field, and in half an hour she will be back, clucking the brood together, weaving in and out of the tall grass very much like a domestic fowl. Long after they can all fly she will protect them in this way. In early October she may still trail a seemingly broken wing and invite death from the gun as she flies up and alights close at hand.

The real poacher does not bother much with the partridge. For one thing, the price of a partridge hardly repays the effort and guile required to come by one, and, for another, the hunting of a partridge must be done across an open field, arable land close to the farm.

Francie McGinn is a man fond of shooting partridges. He will go striding down a field of swedes or across a harvest field in a hurry, ready to shoot at the first movement, alert for the bounding rabbit, the running hare or the rising partridge. When he puts them up his gun will swing in a smooth movement, and almost always two will cease to fly in flight with the others and begin to roll and tumble through the air in a curve ending on the ground. The feathers they shed will still be drifting in the air after he has lifted them and hurried on for the boundary.

A man can become known as a poacher more quickly through shooting partridges than any other way. The farmer takes an interest in the covey and counts them. They are a thing he enjoys for his supper on a Sunday evening. Just like the poachers who will exchange information on the subject, he will remark, "I notice there's only three in the covey on the little hill to-day. Did you see anybody about after them?" You saw the stoat hunting through the grass, halting and rearing, showing off the light hair on his belly, sniffing and turning his head, cunning and vicious. No, the stoat did not get them. The cock and hen are wary. They too, raise their heads. They hear the rustle of the grass. Perhaps they get the odour of the stoat as well as the scent of the red clover. When they go, they move unobtrusively, hurrying across the bare patches with heads down, moving with new dignity when they cross the soft earth among the round rushes, upright, promenading, taking time to pick at an insect or a seed. The stoat did not get them, nor the cat. Perhaps the little owl, flying silently at nightfall, like a shadow, a ghost? Perhaps the little owl dropped among them? You saw the patch of scattered feathers? The brown and white feathers that form a heart on the breast of the bird? It might have been a bird of prey, for the carcase is gone, and there is no other sign but the feathers rolling and turning in the light wind, but more likely it was the crepuscular poacher who heard the cry and hastened over the brow to try a shot against the mottled sky of nightfall.

59

I have known poachers to keep a record of the number of birds in a covey and to hunt the covey at every opportunity until all the birds were in the hand of the dealer. Yesterday I heard of a poacher who sells them for three shillings and sixpence each and sometimes four shillings. Not so many years ago a hare was worth no more than two shillings—and partridges? I cannot remember, but pigeons were two for sixpence and now they are half a crown!

The dealer will turn the brace in his hand, pinch the breasts and click his lips.

"Poor things, these," he will say. "What price you want for these? They're no more than sparrows!"

You will name your price and remember that it makes no difference. Refuse, and he will tell the policeman you offered him game, and the policeman will ask to see your licence to shoot game. As though the fraternity concerned itself with licence! It is the very lack of licence that makes poaching. A man takes a licence for his mongrel, then a licence for his gun and the next thing he knows he is asking permission to shoot. When he is refused he is a poacher no more, but a tame villager who is in bed when the church clock strikes ten, every night of the week without exception!

Take the dealer's price. There was some reward in coming by the partridge. Some skill and cunning and not a little risk.

Getting a pair of partridges may take a poacher more time than he has to spare. The wind carried the sound of his approach and up rose the covey and away it went over the dome of the green hill; all at once one of the hens came out between two lumps of gorse and saw him before he was in gunshot, and her flight brought the rest winging after her, away across the meadow, diminishing in size and blending with the slope to which they sank with stretched wings and out-thrust necks. Little Hugh would lean over the gate and listen to the call of the cock bird, then look at the sky and nod his head, deciding to go for the net in a little while when the light had less strong reflection on the whitewash of the farm buildings and the first little glimmer of oil-lamps was showing in the windows of the village.

On the harvest field, where the clover aftergrowth is thick, the rabbits are almost buried. They have only to crouch and they are hidden. The man advancing only knows where they have hidden when the leaves of the clover hiss and flutter at the rabbit's frantic passage. In such growth the partridges could not feel safe to roost. Perhaps they are there when the sunlight is bright at mid-day and the leaves are dancing and the clover blossoms swaying, but towards evening, when their crops are full and they draw closer together for the night, they prefer the shorter grass of the pasture. On this field they can see the movement of the sheep and the grazing horse. The ploughman, short-cutting to his cottage, clumps past ten yards from them and they sit tight, almost vanishing into the ground. The stoat works his way along the bank, slinking into one burrow and out of another and misses their scent, or, if he finds them, they take a short flight in a half circle, alight and run a few yards, then walk with heads raised as they watch for sign of pursuit. The stoat lets them go, for he would wear himself away in chasing them. They close in again and seem to settle for the night. The owl glides out over the field in a slow, sinking wheel after a mouse or a vole and the partridges sit there like miniature chickens.

Hang on the gate, like Little Hugh. Let the light wane and the bat begin to fly about under the trees. Listen to the hollow sounds of twilight and mark the spot where the partridges settled when their brief walk ended. There they are, between the dead thistle and the tall weed. That little patch of uncropped grass, no deeper than the probe of a man's finger, hides all

eight of them. A riddle would cover the lot of them. Begin, even now, to walk towards them and they will run or rise from the ground like an eruption, so sudden, so expected and yet unexpected, that its sound will startle you and they will be gone, settled somewhere else in the enfolding dusk. Look at the waterlogged ground in the hollow. When it is black and no longer reflects light; when you cannot tell whether the shadow across the hill is a fox on his run or a hare bumping slowly over to the deeper gloom of the boundary hedge, they will sit still and make no attempt to move, unless your misguided feet carry you into the roosting place.

The netting of partridges is more often talked about than successfully carried out. It is not hard where the place in which they roost is clear of the hedge so that a man can walk between the covey and the hedge without disturbing the birds, when there are no little clumps of gorse, dead docks or hazel rods stuck in the ground to foul the net. It is not hard where a feeding rabbit does not rise and dash right through the covey. It is so easy under these circumstances that where they exist the partridges do not!

Every poacher with a reputation will give you his way of netting partridges. Remember the covey sits still in the dark. A rabbit will run and a hare too, but a partridge is snug in the darkness. A careless searcher would mistake its feather blending in daylight. In the night it is safe, so it need not run unless the thing disturbing it is close at hand, and then it will hurl itself into the air, into the vast space of night where you have no more hope of netting it than the curlew that flies high in the darkness making its lonely cry. Mark the spot, they will tell you, and look out for the obstacles placed in the field to prevent netting, the thorn branch and the gorse fragment to become entangled in the net being drawn across the field. Look out for the sheep, the ewe and her grown lamb dashing side by side between you and your companion. Let three of you go, they will advise, and the third man can disentangle the net, lifting it over the obstacles so that progress can go on.

This I can advise, for I have tried my hand at the art: the fewer engaged in the job, the quieter will be its execution, so let no more than three of you go. You have marked the roosting place. Take the twenty-five-yard net that hangs in the stable or the shed. Examine it in daylight, see that your weights are tied along one side of it, then, at nightfall, carry it stretched between you, holding it as taut as you can. At every step you will know if the tight net has encountered a thistle or a twig. Draw it high at first, then draw it lower as you approach your landmarks, the dark shadow of the hollybush in the hedge, the fence-post in the other boundary. As the net comes the covey may try to rise. You will feel it all and learn how to handle the net. It is not easy. A fool can put a rabbit out of a burrow with a ferret but it takes a wildfowler to net partridges. Like netting a hare, it is a thing that is either successful or a complete failure. The expedition begins at nightfall and it is over before the farm dog has stopped his barking, before the fox has crossed from the thicket to the wood. At its end you have either a covey in your bag or you have nothing but a point or two to add to experience!

Little Hugh, a man of great patience, will have his net in readiness. He will decide whether the birds settled where he saw them last or ran for the engulfing gorse. When he has considered all these things he will put his feet in seed bags to muffle his boots and bid you do the same. He will speak no more until it is all over, and there will be no dog either at your heels or his own! You will know Little Hugh well before you share this enterprise with him. When it is over he wants the birds in his hands and to ensure it you will have to co-ordinate your movements with his, understand what he is doing without seeing him, become a poacher in the true meaning of the word.

These are the only ways I know of getting partridges: use a gun or a net, or, like Black Bill, blow a whistle or fly a kite so that they keep to the ground to be taken by walking up and shooting. Anton, as I have said, will set traps. I heard of a man who put little steel traps in the dust where partridges were in the habit of taking a bath, fluffing their feathers and basking in the sun. There are cruel ways and ways less cruel. Partridges are such handsome, dignified little birds that it seems a pity to harm them. They are preserved as game because they are tasty on the plate and slaughtered by the dozen couple when the shooting party goes through the turnips and over the hill. It is said that they are a difficult shot and fly very fast with the wind. The poacher never shoots a dozen couple or nets half that number. He takes what the fox might take, what the hunting stoat might take, by wits and cunning and with less regularity. To him, as Little Hugh might say, they are no one's birds until they are in the hand of him who can catch them.

I remember watching a covey on a September day. It had been very hot and I was in the cool of the farm kitchen, seated in my grandfather's arm-chair and gazing idly out of the window at the little field where the beehives sat. Among the beehives I suddenly saw the movement of a partridge. It was so near the house that I caught my breath with surprise. The hen partridge led her brood through the white bee-boxes and down the grass past the chickens that were sitting in their hollows at the hedge bottom. The guinea-fowl ignored them and a cat sprawled on the grass looked at them and went on washing its paws with its tongue. I thought of Sunday evening supper and looked at the gun leaning against the clock. All at once my attention was taken by the partridges again. A long-legged, scrawny chicken stalked slowly towards the covey. As she drew near the hen partridge she shot out her neck and pecked. The partridge ran and the covey followed at her heels. The chicken gave chase. Round the first beehive they went. The partridges twisted and turned in unison. It seemed as though they were tied together by fine thread. The winding chase went on for a minute or two and then the covey seemed to tire of the game, for as one they rose and threw themselves over the stone wall in a short flight that left the domestic fowl frustrated. When I went out with the gun a little later they were gone and I was glad.

IF the rabbit is the bread and butter of the poacher, then the pheasant completes his diet. The ways of coming by a pheasant are numerous and legendary. Some of the ways are dangerous and some of them are ways practised by poachers only when they have an ale pot in their hands and a warm glow inside. When I was a youth the keeper in the locality was convinced that I shot sackfuls of his pheasants in a season, and told our neighbours that he had seen me knocking his birds down time and time again; but I was sixteen and he was seventy. There was truth in the difference in our ages, but he had cunning and experience if I had fleetness of foot, and I always felt I owed it to him to do my best to make his exaggeration of sackfuls of pheasants less of a lie than it was. We developed a strong mutual hatred of each other. He would send messages to me through a relative.

"Tell him," he would say, "I saw him Tuesday afternoon on the turnip hill. I saw him put the cock down. If I catch him he's for the court!"

To my disgust and shame, my relative who was friendly with the keeper would give me a lecture on the errors of my ways and the danger I ran. These lectures had little effect. I shot nearer and nearer the keeper's lodge, where he had a wire-netting enclosure in which he fed a number of almost tame birds. One day, in defiance, I took a shot at a group of birds through the netting, believing the keeper to be away elsewhere on the estate. The shot was not so much intended to kill pheasants as to give the keeper news of my boldness through his wife, who was in her garden at the time. The report of my gun had hardly died when the lodge door flew open and the keeper came lumbering out. I turned and ran. Somehow he drew closer than I had expected and I found myself running uphill in a firwood with the old man about seventy yards behind. Before I reached the top I slipped and tumbled back. The distance between us shortened alarmingly. I could see him panting up after me as I clawed myself upright and tried to run again. Perhaps he had exhausted himself and saw that, close though we were, he could never overtake me; perhaps he grew desperate and more enraged by the feebleness of his years, but as I scrambled on I heard the roar of his gun and a second or so later I felt something strike my neck. No rabbit was ever more frightened. I fell and put my hand to my head. I hardly dared look at it to see the blood from the gunshot wound, but when I looked I saw my hand was not marked by my blood as I feared. New heart came to me. Before he could fire again I was through the trees at the top of the ride and going like a deer down the other side, leaping over gaping warrens and roots, escaping as I had done countless times before. The spattering feeling on my neck had been caused by fragments of fir twigs coming down upon me as the keeper's shot tore through the trees high above!

Two friends of mine who were chased by a keeper ran through a park carrying a gun and a sack containing four birds, and were accompanied by their lurcher. When a second keeper joined the first, and a car began to race ahead of them down an adjoining drive, it seemed certain that they would be caught. One swung round and ran off at right angles to the original flight, and the other turned to give battle. The two keepers separated. The running poacher, who carried the sack and gun, became the quarry of one of the keepers. The poacher who stood his ground gave a signal to his dog. It ran in quickly and snapped at the heel of the keeper's boot and over he went. The second keeper hesitated, and the poacher broke back past him. He turned to give chase and the lurcher somehow ran in between his legs and brought him down as he had the other. The first poacher was by now well into the shelter of a near-by wood. His companion whistled up the dog with two fingers and ran on, and soon he too was in cover. The same evening when I met them they were laughing about the dog. It seemed that the dog had been taught the game by the children of one of them, and had become a bugbear in the village for the habit of up-ending anyone who ran or moved fast. It sobered them both a little when I remarked that it was a good thing the dog had not chosen to turn playful with either of them while the keepers were in chase.

It is not an exaggeration to say that on some estates the keeper has his pheasants counted. He walks through a field in the late afternoon and watches the cock and his plurality of hens running for cover. He makes a note of one cock and four hens in the thicket in the hollow. Next week he may note that he has gathered another hen. He will also note that the cock came out alone when he walked through the thicket and that two odd hens got up from the blackberry tangle on the far slope into the hollow. It reads like a book to his experienced eye. They have scattered, badly disturbed, and perhaps two hens have fallen. Certainly one has gone, for he saw the wad of a cartridge on the open field and a few yards away some feathers sticking in the mud, and the imprint of a hobnailed boot.

The whole world is quiet, blanketed with chill mist. In among the beech trees the leaves are damp. The thick barrier of the spruce-planting gives out a resinous smell. Out on the green of the field the pheasants are feeding, a short run from the dead bracken, so near a matching shade for the plumage of a hen or a cock pheasant.

The keeper hangs about. Yesterday at half-past three he heard the report of a gun. He is in the clear patch below the towering dead tree. Like the pheasant, his dress is a blend with the brown and grey of the wood. He hears the fence creak and the little sound that might have been a man coughing into his hand. The pheasants hear it too. They are no longer picking among the grass. The cock bird has his head

raised and the hens are intent on the small sounds and vibrations. They do not run. There seems to be no hurry, but they fade from the field. They are in the bracken, steering through the fallen elm and the debris of broken branches, up over the bank that is riddled with rabbit holes and on under the awning of bracken that has fallen on other dead branches and twigs.

The poacher is on the far side of the field, a figure hard to see, for he is standing close to the oak tree with a hawthorn behind him. He did not see the pheasants go off the field. He looked for them within yards of the spot on which they fed, but his eye caught

71

the pigeon gliding out over the fringe of the wood and he saw it loop up and go in fast flight back in the direction from which it came. It was all too far away for him to have seen the keeper or his dogs, or for the pigeon to have sighted him by the oak tree, although the pigeon has eyes keener than the hawk. The pigeon was no more than a dot. To the man who has not studied the characteristic flight of birds it might have looked like a pigeon, a crow, a magpie or even a fieldfare. Its turn in flight from a glide to fast-beating wings could have indicated a hundred things and none of them the right thing, but the poacher knew in that instant where the keeper stood, and the keeper knew too, when he heard the clatter of the pigeon's wings, that if the pigeon had been observed, the poacher was moving away with the same noiseless stealth as the pheasants.

The poaching of a pheasant by day is a thing of stealth or great speed. The wind is blowing and making the whole wood rock. It has blown since the earliest hours of the morning. The crossed limbs of an ash and gangling thorn squeak and groan, and dead fir-cones rain on the grass and the path. The pigeons, carried across the undulating country by the buffeting wind, sweep in and take bobbing foothold on the top branches of tall trees from which they can keep watch. They are more nervous because in the wind the warning is carried away unheard. They love the hollow stillness of the watery sunset when the smallest noise resounds through the drum of the wood. Now they sway aloft there until they tire of their vigilance and take a short heavy flight to the sea of thick fir-tops.

Like the pigeon, the pheasant loves the echoes, and the quiet day when the tractor purrs a mile away and the sound of children playing about the farm carries clearly across the acres of sleeping land.

On this day, with the wind making your eyes sting and its hands plucking at your clothes, take the shortest route across the fields and hurry along the hedge-side. That gully round which the three elms stand is a likely spot. The pheasant cock with his attendant hens went down to the little stream, moving through the two patches of gorse. The last dead leaf comes whirling past you as you go towards the trees. Put your finger on the hammers and gently ease them back so that both triggers are cocked. Get ready. It is a strange thing, but somehow at the instant of your appearance they will know you are there and become for a moment so motionless that you will not see them though they are in the centre of your vision. Their rising will not coincide with your own coming to life. Put up the gun and shoot, right, left, and the thump you heard was one of them striking the ground behind the gorse. Hurry forward with the dog, for the bird may only be winged, and already racing up the knoll and over to the cover of the wood and its undergrowth.

Study the pheasant and his habits. Early in the morning, when the sun is a streak of light in the east and day is only half-arrived, with the fox no more than settled in his lair, the pheasant moves gingerly out over the old wheat stubble. There is no gamebird with hearing like his. In the growing light he feeds, walks a little way, listens and walks again, and cover is always close at hand. When he is with his harem he will be lulled a little, and venture farther into the open field, but split from them, perhaps by the last raid of the shooting party, he will be cautious. No nervous hen will save him the anxiety of having to take a morsel and listen twice. Watch him from the shelter of the hazel copse and the screen of blackthorn draped with rakings from the side of a harvest cart. When he vanishes you will know that you betrayed yourself by some unconscious movement that carried warning in sound so small that you could not believe it would reach him. Walk out with your eyes fixed on the spot where he was. If he can see you as well as hear you, he will run a few feet and launch himself into the air with great speed and sound of thrashing wings. He will look heavy and a grand target until you miss him. If he does not see you he will stay where he is until you are almost on top of him, or until you have blindly walked past, and then he will go with a suddenness that will paralyse your movements while he puts yards between you and his magnificent red, white and chestnut-brown body.

In the afternoon, in the scent of mustard and swedes, you will see him for a brief instant between the rows, the spear of his outline vanishing between leaves that flutter and bob and rustle. You will begin to walk. Every stride will make you more excited, and while you walk he will run. At the end of the field he will speed up the bank and into the tangle of rose and honeysuckle, and on, over the cart-track, never bothering to reveal his escape by the noise of his wings.

In the undergrowth of the thicket you will be startled by the sudden rustling of leaves and a scurrying like a rabbit breaking out. This is not the habit of the rabbit. When you are close and he is in cover, he crouches, and, when you have moved a little way he hurries noiselessly off, but the pheasant cock becomes uncomfortable at your proximity and runs. You have little hope of seeing him. In a moment he is in the dry ditch and away without more sound, or the rustling passes into the next clump of briar and dead bracken, across the wet ground where the alder grows, and over the leaves and beech mast, and ends with the whirr of his wings and the alarm call sounding across the adjoining field.

Hurry to the fence. He towers yonder above the stunted ash and the elderberry, and then drops, yes, drops for all the world like a hen fluttering heavily from a spar. The undergrowth is thick about him. He runs downhill now, across the mouth of the badger hole, past the badger "hay" that lies where the badger scratched it out when last he cleaned house, under the drooping nightshade and past the wild raspberry canes, until the memory of your intrusion in the thicket grows faint and he begins to pause, pick and listen once more.

At dusk he will come out of the tangle, for his scent is strong, and the fox is hungrier when the frost is in the late autumn air. His enemies would find him and he could not outrun them, or rise, for the tangle above would bring him down to the snapping jaws of the grizzled badger or the fox. Before it is too dark he will take flight again, across to the thicket or the firwood, and fly into the lower branches of the tree to roost. There he is, not so high as the pigeon or the crow

75

perhaps, but you must learn to recognise him and distinguish him from the old nest of the rook, the thorny nest-renovation of the magpie and the thick growth that afflicts some trees. The gloom below is a comfort to him. Night settles in about the fir tree, the holly bush and the thorn, and he is safe.

Some of the boldest characters are those who poach pheasants, for it requires boldness both by night and by day, unless you have the gift of Black Bill and the cunning of Little Hugh. It was always said of a keeper I knew that he spent the night in bed when a gang of local poachers conveyed the information that they would be after pheasants. The landlord would lean across the bar and in a confidential whisper tell him, "Some o' that lot is after the birds to-night. Thought I'd better tell you." The keeper would nod his head and scowl, then go quickly out to his bicycle and ride home, so that if official warning came in the night he could always give the poachers a chance to get away by the fact that he had to dress and put on his boots before giving chase! Gangs of poachers, banded together for protection and a large return in cash, do not hesitate to fight their way out of a tight corner, and if a gun goes off in the dark, it may be aimed either at a roosting pheasant or the keeper of the pheasants!

Black Bill, whose eye missed nothing, never failed to get pheasants without a gun. His method was an old one. In the middle of a small wood he would construct his own hedge of sturdy twigs. These would be set so close together that they formed an impenetrable wall for a pheasant, but at intervals he would leave small gaps and in these gaps he would hang nooses, or small snares. When the thing was nicely constructed and the snares set, he would go home. The following morning he would return to beat through the wood with the sound-making device of two sticks which he struck against each other. The pheasants on his side of the barrier would run quietly and unseen to the twigs and dart through the gaps to be snared as neatly as rabbits. When he lifted his catch and reset his wires he would make a wide circuit of the wood and enter it again from the other end, tapping his sticks and walking to the long barrier. In this way he would clear almost every pheasant that did not rise and fly. Not only would Black Bill set wires in an artificial hedge, but he observed the runs of pheasants, the places where they passed through a natural hedge, going under a branch or through a clump of bracken.

Little Hugh had an old shotgun cut down for the purpose of shooting roosting pheasants. He would take this abbreviated gun, easily concealed because of its shorter barrels and trimmed stock, and creep into a wood at nightfall. When there was no moon he would use a torch, flashing it on and directing its beam into a likely tree. The gun having been cut off at the pistol grip of the stock, he could use in the same way as a pistol, which enabled him to hold the torch in one hand and aim with the other. He was very proud of this method until he was caught and his gun confiscated.

I remember the first time I tried by moonlight. I shot three old crows one after the other, and dared not remain in the wood any longer because the intervals between my shots had given the keeper ample time to locate me.

Go with Little Hugh. He will impress upon you that you must keep your ears open, that you must not mistake an owl for a pheasant, or shoot unless you are sure. He will hold the light and direct your shot because he knows where to look. You might go to the bleak north side of the planting or the open trees, the tall and bare beeches and elms, but Little Hugh will take you to places where he knows the birds roost, and his knowledge is from observation as well as instinct. The shadow in the tree is one of his specialities. When the torch goes on and you fire, a pheasant will fall or Little Hugh will seek an accomplice who "shapes like the thing".

The first time you take a share of a bag you will want to eat one yourself, and this may lead to your undoing. The feathers, blowing about your garden will give you away to the keeper, so you must hide them. Pluck

79

the bird into a bucket of water, dig a hole and pour the soaked feathers into the earth and cover them over with soil. Once, knowing the importance of hiding game feathers, I plucked a bird into the fire. The following day I suffered anxiety because pheasant feathers blew round about the house, on the garden path and among the leaves of our privet hedge! They had been carried up the chimney by the hot draught in the flue and spilled themselves down the roof for the whole world to know I had been poaching again!

With a keeper hard on my heels I once bolted into the farm kitchen, carrying my gun and a brace of birds. I looked desperately round for a hiding place, knowing that the keeper, although he had no right to do such a thing, might dash into the room after me. One of my aunts, anxious for my good name, and with a little of the family devil in her, perhaps, pulled open the door of the grandfather clock. I dropped the brace inside, laid the gun in its usual corner and flopped in a chair at the moment the keeper knocked loudly on the door.

Hospitality had never been refused even our greatest enemy. My aunt opened the door and invited the keeper in without asking why he was so out of breath and red of face. Would he have a cup of tea? I controlled my breathing a little better and bade him good-day in what I thought to be a casual voice.

"Pheasants?" I asked.

He blustered and accused. I brazenly said he could search if he wished, but he stalked out, rudely refusing the tea my aunt offered. He had hardly crossed the threshold when the weight of the clock ran down, and instead of striking the bottom board with a crash it softly thudded on to the pheasants!

On another occasion the same keeper paid my grandfather a visit and sat on our settle-bed. Under him, hastily transferred out of sight from the hook in the ceiling-boards, were two partridges and a hen pheasant. As a rule, however, game was kept out of sight in the long, cold cupboard under the stairs where my grandmother matured her blackberry and elderberry wine. There was even a time when I became so notorious that gun and cartridges were kept there too, and the story went about that my grandfather had sold the gun to force me to mend my ways.

While on the subject of hiding places for birds and the disposal of feathers, remember that pheasant or partridge are better hidden up from the ground. Tie their feet together and hang them on the coat-hook, covered by an old jacket. Your dog or the dog of a visitor will be less likely to scent them up there, for the air rises from the floor and carries the scent to the ceiling.

Whatever bird you shoot, you will learn a great deal about his current feeding habits by examining his crop. Look at the crop of the pigeon. He is on the stubble of the wheat in September, among the oaks and full of acorns in October, nibbling at bits of green stuff and hedge berries later and among the first shoots in early spring, the sprouting pea and the "bread and cheese" of the hawthorn. In the same way you may learn where the partridge searches for food, and the fact that the pheasant is being fed wheat or oats in some sheltered glade known only to the keeper. Wherever the pheasant lives there will be water, a streamlet or a ditch, cover close at hand. Like the keeper, you can set up as a feeder of game. Get yourself a small bag of corn and fatten your birds as Little Hugh and other poachers like to do.

Baiting the ground is an old and favoured way of getting game. The keeper does it to ensure birds in certain parts of the estate just before a shoot is to take place, and if it works for the keeper, it works as well for the poacher. A bag of tail corn left by the thrashing mill is good enough for attracting pheasants, but it must be scattered in a suitable place, perhaps along the side of a wood or in bare patches in a stony hollow where the birds have been seen on a bright autumn day. Like snaring, or prowling the wood in the moonlight, it has its dangers. The keeper knows that corn and chaff does not come into a lonely field at the back of a hill by accident. He knows where the pheasants are, and in such places he makes his rounds, so that when you bait ground with corn it is as well to reconnoitre the locality every time before making another sowing.

Francie's method would be to lay the corn for several days until a good enough number of birds were congregated to feed there, and then he would creep up with his gun and let go both barrels into the thickest mass, hoping to kill three or four. Little Hugh, as great an expert in another method, would change his bait on the last day and return in time to lift his intoxicated pheasants.

I have not seen this carried out, but I know the potent effect of a drop of spirit on a canary! We had a canary once. He sang all day long in a cage above my grandfather's chair and his song was taken for granted, while, like the collie dog and the black horse, he grew old. One day it was noticed that he had a "wheeze" in his chest and the next he took to falling off the spar. A drop of whisky worked wonders for any member of the family who caught cold. Might it not work wonders for Joey? One drop in his water dish and Joey revived. Two drops for insurance, as it were, and Joey became intoxicated, swayed and closed his eyes and generally behaved like an inebriated canary. Often I have promised myself that I will try making pheasants drunk, but baiting requires patience not to be wasted by any method likely to prove sterile in results.

Black Bill, the man with the way of birds, always knew a novel method. He would bait under cover, in the tunnel between a thorn hedge and a field of gorse, in the shelter of a hazel copse, among the dead grass and sleeping roots of primrose and wood anemones. His bait would be corn and raisins, and after the second or third day there would be more raisins and less corn, with a fish-hook in every raisin! A pheasant must be able to raise its head in order to take off. It cannot fly if its head is held to the ground by a short length of brown line attached to a rod. Black Bill would fasten ten or a dozen hooks to a rod. Walking among the grass in search of grain and the tasty raisins it had yesterday, the pheasant would take the raisin and hook in an instant and remain attached to the rod until Black Bill called back. There is cruelty and cunning in this method. The bird which swallowed the bait could not escape with the raisin in its crop, nor could it disgorge it without drawing away from the rod. When this happened the hook would slip through the raisin and fasten itself in the lining of the crop so that escape would become impossible.

There are two other ways belonging to the legends on taking pheasants. I have heard of both of them often enough without ever coming across the man who has actually used one or the other of them. Perhaps he died a long time ago, or did he only have an hour of glory when those about him gaped as he expounded his cunning?

"Ah," they will say, "there's more ways of killin' a cat than feedin' it on cream. . . ."

If you are to believe this story and prove the effectiveness of the method, you bait the ground with wheat or hard peas. When the birds have become accustomed to feeding in your selected spot, go to the stable and pull some of the long hairs from the mane of the mare. Watch she does not turn and snap at you as you jerk them out! The hairs are selected with some care. They must be long enough and stiff enough. A hole is made in the grain or the pea by means of a pin or a fine needle and the hair threaded through this hole. Every piece of bait is threaded on to a strand of hair and the bagful taken and scattered where yesterday's bait was laid. The voracious pheasant will gobble down the first grain of wheat or pea, and the hair will protrude from his beak. He will gulp and wipe his beak on the ground, strike at it with his foot, first the right foot and then the left. The urgency to remove the hair will become desperation and in the end the pheasant will fall down, still striking at his beak in a frenzy until he is exhausted. The poacher will return in the afternoon and find his birds lying about, unable to fly, unable to rise, incap-

able of anything except the feeblest kicking of one leg at a head that distinctly wobbles! They can be lifted and bagged with ease!

I do not guarantee this method. Some ways of coming by a rabbit, pheasant, partridge or hare require skill, and some, like that of sending a tortoise down a burrow bearing a lighted candle-stump on its back, so that it may drive out rabbits, require no more than credulity.

The second method, and I cannot vouch for it, or even claim an acquaintance who has used it, is the use of rock sulphur. The poacher buys a quantity of sulphur and puts it into a large tin in the sides of which he has punched a number of holes. The sulphur can is carried to a wood. The moon must shine or the poacher must have a torch or lantern. There must be a good breeze, not a wind, for it would defeat the object. The sulphur is set on fire, and the can or cans are placed so that the fumes carry on the breeze into the trees. A whiff of sulphur fumes will overcome a pheasant in a minute or two and the poacher has no more to do than to pick them off the ground, having thrown a sack over his gas-producing outfit.

For my part, I have always favoured the straightforward way of getting a pheasant: a shot and a walk in the shelter of a tall hedge or through a wood.

In the idle days, when the poacher has no income and has to concern himself with a day at harrowing or muck-spreading, cleaning a ditch or burning couch grass, the partridges are pairing and flying in pairs, rising quickly and sailing over hedges in short flights, and the cock pheasant is gathering his complement of young hens. Yesterday, when the wheatear was on the harrowed furrow, the pheasant rose from the hedgeside and went down in the thicket in the hollow. The late lambs have come, and the bluebells are in the wood where there is warmth and crackle of heat that makes the man on the footpath think of the gliding grass snake and the basking adder. The pheasant is nesting. There, in the clump of gorse, by the tangle

86

of old fence wire and the stones gathered from the field to fill an idle afternoon, the hen sits tight on a nest of fawn eggs. See the proud and richly marked cock going down across the muddy patch at the brook and those eggs seem small for such a fine bird, particularly after you have seen the sharp-pointed large egg of the curlew, or even the plover's clutch on the brown earth where the oats were sown. The hen pheasant has her eggs and the cock leaves her for some new fancy in his harem. Go near the nest and she will desert. How often will you find a nest of blue-stained, rotten eggs when the hay is cut down. Perhaps the country boy, on his journey with a ladle of oats to lure a pony off a hill, found the nest by accident, moved the grass, disturbed the place and made her forsake.

I remember finding such a nest. It was in the shelter of a gorse bush and when I found it the hen was sitting. She must have been paralysed in broody fever as some birds seem to be, for she did not rise. I could not resist touching her. I stroked the wonderful smoothness of her back and hastened to bring my grandmother to see what I had found. I was thoroughly scolded for interfering with the hen, but two days later I crept back. The nest was there and the eggs too, every one as cold as the stones which lay about.

There was a time when the keeper would pay for information as to the whereabouts of pheasant nests. Make a journey to his cottage and he would give a shilling when he had confirmed the information. Usually the country lad would milk the nest of three or four eggs before telling the keeper. Once I met a

87   G

bird-nester who carried a great pan-basket filled with the eggs of partridge and pheasant. I wonder now whether he knew the old way of testing an egg by seeing whether it would sink or swim, and knowing that if it sank it was not addled.

At the corner of the street leading into the town square a character known as Butcher Murphy propped a wall on most days. The Butcher was a noted poacher. I never heard of his being caught. His skill and cunning were well known. When he was missing, it was said that he had made an expedition after game. He always fired his shot from the road and concealed his gun in his clothes. When our trap turned into the main street, where we called on the saddler or the ironmonger, Butcher Murphy would give us good-day. His moustache straggled on his lip and added to his swarthy appearance. There was a glint in his eye, too, that made me consider him as an able man, one who could teach the rest a thing or two, one who knew more than he said.

I imagined, as I held the pony and waited until my grandfather had done his business with the merchant, that Butcher Murphy looked at the trees in the square, listened to the rooks quarrelling, and thought of a turn in the road where pheasants fed in the stubble or partridges went boldly up a stony brow, just clear of the hedge in his line of fire. When he bowed his head and spat between his boots he was thinking of the moves. The cart that was jolting along the road had swung slowly out of sight, the man "looking" sheep had whistled in his dog and sunk behind the hill. The servant girl on her bicycle pushed self-consciously on her pedals and went round the bend, and Butcher Murphy took the gun out of his clothes, the shortened barrels from his trouser-leg, the stock from the lining of his jacket and the fore-end from his pocket. Now the muffled click of the gun's assembling and the breach closing on the cartridges. One bright, sharp eye closing as the gun pointed at the feeding birds.

That corner was Butcher Murphy's corner. When I was small he was there, and when I had grown to manhood he was still there, unchanged, for all I could notice. The dog on the path before the Italian's ice-cream parlour might be a different dog, but it was the same corner and the same Butcher Murphy with his knowing look, a look that appealed to my imagination and made me want to know the secrets of Butcher Murphy, a thing I never knew at first hand, though gossip told enough to keep me for ever interested.

"Who was about the town to-day?" they would ask at home.

"This one and that one, and Butcher Murphy on the corner."

It was when he was not there that his reputation was made.

A while ago I met a man who had only poached once in his life and his method was the strangest I have ever heard. Owen drove a van for a country butcher in the days before motor vans buzzed round the farms and villages. He was sitting up behind his horse, letting the tired creature take its time on a long hill, when he saw ahead of him three pheasants feeding on a bank above the road. There was plenty of time

89

to think. Owen looked for a weapon. There was no loose stone by the roadside. He had no hidden gun, but his eye caught his whip. At a distance of a few yards from the feeding birds, he drew up the horse and stepped quietly down on to the grass verge. Somehow the movement of a horse, or even a man on foot on a road, does not excite a feeding bird or animal. Perhaps, like the crow pitching in the wind

on the top of a roadside elm, they know that the stretch of road is a thing apart from the pasture and the business of the man on the road differs from that of the man on the field. Owen crawled up the bank without a sound. The hen pheasant nearest to him jerked up her head in alarm and in that instant the whip cracked out and coiled itself about her neck and she scrambled and fluttered on the grass. The cock and the other hens burst into flight as Owen threw himself on to the top of the bank and grabbed the hen

90

before she could become disentangled and take flight. The practised hand of the butcher's man quickly wrung her neck, and, when the horse began its journey again and Owen leant forward on his seat to replace his whip, the pheasant lay behind him under the canvas.

Every expedition in pursuit of game has something to mark it in memory: the rabbit that got away leaving only two tufts of hair to mark a near miss, the hailstorm that lashed the valley and made the leaves dance, the impudent fox that stood for a minute scratching itself before going through the hedge, the mixed bag in the snow when the woodcock, stockdove and widgeon kept company with the rabbit and the jack snipe. My first outing after a wild duck is a memory as vivid as any I possess. The rain had set in early in the afternoon, and a mist from the hills hung close above the fields. While I was crossing the farmyard three ducks came over low, flying one above the other. I stared at them, and as they vanished, I knew that they were off to feed in the waterholes of the moss. Hastening to the house, I rummaged in the drawer for four-shot cartridges, took down oilskins and lifted the gun. In half an hour I had crossed our march fence and was out across the moss, skirting the peat sloughs and the patches of green weed. No duck rose.

I went on and on with the light fading and the cry of high-flying curlews seeming muffled and far away. At length I came to more solid ground, a little hill with gorse dotted about and the paths of sheep crisscrossing it. I stopped. Right before me, no more than twelve feet from me, was the handsomest drake I had ever beheld. He was an immaculate bird of green, brown, fawn, blue, black and white. The drake feathers at his tail curled beautifully. The sheen on him could only have been painted. He stood, his head raised, his eye bright and the white brands on his neck and wings showing. I caught my breath. There was an age that was yet no more than two deep sighs, and then he gave a quack and flapped into the air. I stood wondering whether I had seen a farmyard drake take flight or a mallard going off in search of a new and safer feeding ground. How easily I could have destroyed him and how hard it was to explain why I had not attempted to lift my already cocked gun!

Something of the same happened to me on the one and only occasion when a red deer was within range. I had strayed from the arable fields of an uncle's farm after three hares that had frolicked through a little wood to the edge of a drained bog. Losing the hares in tall grass and round rushes that grew near a cluster of willows, I was walking over the heaving bog towards more solid ground when a young deer sprang out of the rushes into a small clearing about ten yards ahead. I could not move. My hands and arms stiffened and my heart bounded. The deer sniffed, spun round on its back legs and sailed away, bound after bound, into the brown and fawn wilderness, across the peaty drain, through the willow boughs and into the deep gloom of the thicket where the black earth oozed and bubbled, where the tracks of moorhen feet showed on the mud and lily leaves floated on pools. I recovered when the deer had disappeared. I knew that it was useless to follow. The bog would bear the weight of a fleeting deer, an animal well used to the danger spots, but it was a death trap to a slow-moving man.

Although once in a year or two a farmer might find a deer in his turnip field, the wind right, a gun in his hand with the right shot in the cartridge, few deer were ever killed on arable land. Here and there among the farmers, nevertheless, a deerskin rug lay at a bedside. What better place? Where could a man have such a rug that his visitors might not see it, except in his bedroom? Poachers who went after deer waited until the dry weather set in, when the calf was in the willow thicket, lying among the rushes, away in the silence of the waste. Those who had deerskin rugs got them by sneaking in after the calf. The hind would be off, but the calf, helpless little creature, would lie there, twitching an eye as a fly ran over its face, moving its ears anxiously as the prowler with the gun came near. My only glimpses of deer from the "forest moor" were when they dashed away over the hill, leaving a ravaged turnip field.

Going after wild duck I have often spent a long time in very cold water, hiding from the keeper, taking shelter in breast-high rushes and ducking when any wild birds flew over in case the sudden turn of their flight would betray me. Taking a shot at widgeon, I brought one down out in bog where floating islands of reeds drifted and the water flowed through all the growing vegetation, carrying the smallest fragments of green life in its stream. The widgeon fluttered and flapped beyond easy reach. I hated to see it flap away to die slowly and I had no dog. Risking the keeper's eye, I waded out. The widgeon flapped through the rushes. I strode forward. The water rose from my knees to my thighs and then chilled my stomach and waist. Perhaps the widgeon had lured me so that the bog could suck me down, for, when I suddenly became aware of the danger, it stopped flapping, began to swim forward, weaving through the dead wood and water-carried green stuff. The way back taxed my strength and it seemed for a while that the water did not become gradually shallow, although I had not noticed its sudden deepening on my way out. I had hardly got my water-logged boots on hard ground before the keeper clambered over a wall a hundred yards away and I had to run!

In Wales I was in the company of a local poacher when we crossed a farm, to the annoyance of the owner, who waved his stick and urged two sharp-nosed collie dogs after us. Later that day we returned across the same ground, jumping a stream on the way. My companion drew back. I thought he had spotted the owner waiting for us, but, as he held my arm, five or six fat ducks swam round a bend. Up went his gun. Two of the domestic ducks toppled in the water and the rest flapped into the hazels beside the stream. I laughed as he lifted his kill and we hurried on. I remembered my first mallard, and how easily it had escaped me.

Come across the moss after the grouse, the richly coloured red grouse that warns you from the heather shoulder to "goback, goback, goback!" or the black grouse, with his forked tail, so black that he has a tinge of blue about him and little contrasts, the blood-red mark at his eye and the white beneath his tail. Out over the moss, on the edge of the peat hole, the crowing black cock will flutter up and his crowing will stop suddenly as he sees you. There they go, their wings a uniform down-curve as they skim the heather. There seemed to be no breeze, no chance of the birds rising from the ling where they were feeding, and now they have gone. Walk after them and as soon as you appear on a new skyline you will see them again in flight, off into the endless moss with its bog holes and black-faced, lonely-looking sheep.

Francie McGinn would breast the wind, his clothing moulded to his sturdy frame, his dog at his heels the whole time. Let the rabbit go, the odd rabbit of the moss, or the hare that slept out there on the little hill of sun-scorched grass: let them go, Francie would advise. Somehow his winding course over the drier ground would bring him to the layers of the peat cutting. The black cock's startling flight would not spoil his aim and his second shot would be directed at one of the great pack of grouse rising at the crash of the gun.

When you have done this once or twice, perhaps in the morning, or the afternoon when the sun lies low over the heather, you will learn how wary a bird is the black cock and how he sometimes perches in the old thorn tree. Take the bird home and let it hang, for even when it is ready for the pot it will be tough unless it is well cooked. There will be something of the flavour of the moss about him, the strong flavour of the heather roots. There will be the flavour of adventure, too, for out there on the open moor you were as conspicuous as the dead tree and the cairn.

When I think of the wild goose I remember a clear cold morning in late October. I was standing on a hill where I had set snares the previous day, and

gazing across the farmland at the strips of ploughing, the carpet squares of old pasture, stubble going grey, broken and patchy rows of turnips that reminded me of the havoc of the rooks after wireworm in early summer. All at once, in the fields below, the geese thrust up their necks and began to cackle. I could hear the sound faintly and was puzzled for a little while, and then I saw the long formations of the grey lag or pink-footed geese, I could not tell which they were. They came out of the hard sky of the north, no more than dots in V formation. In a little while I heard what the domestic geese had heard, the honking of the wild birds. They came on, high above the hill, and then wheeled, taking direction from their leader and moving with a wonderful co-ordination and precision, to fly towards the great sand flats of the estuary. Long after they were gone the farmyard geese called. There was something pathetic in the call of the heavy, earth-bound birds.

Characters about the town would slip off just before dusk, carrying a variety of ancient guns and hoping to get one shot, or perhaps two, at the wariest of all birds, the wild goose. It was a vigil depending on the wind, the moon climbing at the back of the hill, the glitter of the wet sand and the run of the tide. The man who stood freezing in the cutting wind might see no more than a formation moving against a twilight sky, hear no more than the tinkling notes of the sand birds, the golden plover, the sandpipers, the dunlins, or the hoarse call of a stray wild duck.

Once I took a trip up a river at dusk, watched most of the way by a jealous keeper who hoped to catch me above the high-water mark. The teal and widgeon rose well ahead of me and escaped. The sheldrake, that wonderfully coloured duck that nests in the rabbit hole, and is so salty and fish-flavoured that no one will eat it, evaded me with care that was unnecessary, and when I rounded a bend I came upon a man in a punt with a great cannon clamped in it.

"Look what you've done!" he bawled and rose from the concealment of the rushes as dozens of water birds took wing.

He had been lying there for a long time waiting for enough of the poor creatures to come within range of slaughter. Not long after this I read of a claim of a

97

record number of duck being killed with one shot and I wondered how many more had been killed without being recovered, for a wounded duck often dives and stays below, holding fast to a reed or water weed until it dies.

There is not so much risk to a poacher in going after water birds, for they are not so well preserved. There is not great profit in selling wild duck, for the flesh is dark and not many people like it. The man who goes after duck does it for the love of hunting, just as most poachers shoot a woodcock and put his wing-tip feather in their caps because the shooting of a wood-cock takes skill with a gun. The poacher may be mooching through the wood, looking for a pheasant or letting his dog mark the undergrowth, when the woodcock rises from the mat of dead leaves. Every time a woodcock flies into a wood or out of it, his line of flight is the same, he will swerve past a particular tree and tower out over the tops of others in the same route without variation, but his flight is twisted, rapid wing-beats and a turn. Some of the poachers have a little rhyme they recite, like "Polly put the kettle on", and at the last word the woodcock will twist so that, as soon as he has twisted, he is sighted with the swinging gun and the shot is fired. One winter, in the course of poaching expeditions, I collected sixteen wing-tip feathers and never once had I gone in search of a woodcock. An old man told me that in his youth artists would pay well for these stiff-quilled soft little feathers. I imagine that if they were of use, the artist was asked a good price for them, for there are only two of these feathers to a bird.

Perhaps of all the things in poaching that thrills a man, the narrow escape lives longest in his memory. Once I took hasty refuge in a ditch, where I lay, half covered by a low bridge and an overhanging bush. The farmer, who had called out his labourers to catch me, came and stood on the bridge. I could have touched his boot, and lay in my uncomfortable shelter with a fast-beating heart. The noise of the search died away and it seemed safe to come out, when, for the first time, I realised that I had been under observation throughout the affair. A soldier and a girl had been embracing in the grass on the other side of the ditch. Evidently they thought I was a desperate character, for when I came out, the girl caught nervously at her companion's arm. I looked fiercely at them in case they decided to begin shouting, and made long and fast strides to the nearest cover.

Little Hugh told me that he once took shelter with a companion, lying in the heart of a blackberry tangle. They had been there five minutes when a black spaniel came through the bush and began licking the face of Little Hugh's companion. The man whispered that he had brought an aniseed rag with him so that he could throw it down to distract any dog sent after him! Little Hugh stood up, risking discovery, and taking the rag, threw it with all his strength across the wood, but the spaniel remained until whistled for by its master and it was only by luck that the pair escaped capture!

Lying in shelter, perhaps with head buried in the forest of grass at the hedge bottom, the poacher learns how blind a man can be and how much human sight and real observation depends on movement. If you get out of bed and join the wild characters with the net and the gun you will learn all these things: how to come by the rabbit, the hare, the pheasant, the partridge and, perhaps, a fine or a week or two in prison! The lessons of Black Bill, Little Hugh and Francie McGinn are lessons in nature and the thing is dormant in all of us.

I have got you into bad company and infected you, perhaps, with a restlessness that will take you when your train carries you through wooded country, with the close-growing firs a yard or two from the line, when you catch a glimpse of a bouncing white tail, a countryman plodding over a field in the autumn daybreak. It is not my intention to incite you to get in trouble.

PUT away the gun, the ferret and the dog. Have done with such things. Let me take you to the singing water of the stream, to the deep heavy flow of the river, to study the ripple of the rising trout and hear the plop of the vole launching himself from the bank. Watch the speeding driftwood and the creamy scum that gathers where the trailing thorn rakes the current. In the quietness of the river's course you will come upon the moorhen travelling among the roots of the trees, for ever in search of something, in and out along the bank, through the grass and across the stones. You will come to the broken water over the rocks where the current swirls and bubbles, and here you will see the black and white dipper commit what seems to be suicide by wading into the depths of the flowing water. Up in the water-smoothed rocks you will catch your first glimpse of the salmon, going on, like a ploughing liner, to the sweeter water at the river's source. Here in the deep pool, reflecting the summer sky, you will see the hovering trout or the spurt of gravel where he hovered until you moved. There are secrets in the taking of a fish, secrets known to the boy and the man from the cottage up the road, ways handed down to sons and to the sons of sons. Put away the gun and taste the brown trout, the silvered sea trout, the great salmon.

There is a time when summer is young and the wagtails are nesting by the water, when the flow of the stream slackens and the rocks begin to show. The pools here and there become shallow and the sound of the water dies and the man after a fish forgets how it frothed in colour when the spate of spring roared through the hollows and licked at the top of the bridge's arc. When the water only whispers and sighs and bubbles among the stones the boy from the cottage will come and lie on his stomach and watch the trout. In a little while he will begin dabbling his arms in the water, having dragged his sleeves almost up to his shoulders.

Watch him. He is at the old game of tickling a trout. His hands go feeling in under the belly of the rock. He knows the places where the biggest trout shelter. If you learn to tickle trout you will learn to move your hands in the way you reach for a ferret, without an excited, jerky movement. Smoothly, con-

fidently. The trout, speckled brown and with a cream shade on its under-side almost a match for the delicate old tea rose, will remain motionless, or almost motion-less: a gentle movement of the gills and the slightest balancing against the cold water coming down from the hills. At the coming of the searching fingers he will edge forward a fraction, aware, a little uneasy perhaps, but sure in his knowledge that one move-ment of his tail and fins and he will be off through the pool as fast as the brief reflection of the flying swallow. The hands of the boy are guided by his eyes. He lies sprawled over the rock. One violent motion and he might find himself head first in the pool, but the fingers spread and draw close to the trout. The fish floats higher, closer to the rock. Now the fingers gently reach the under-side of the fish and caress the slipperiness. The trout backs a little. The fingers stroke again and the trout edges back, nervously now, ready to dart away, and the boy waits his time. Now the trout has retreated until the gills are above the fingers and the hands take sudden hold in the only spot a hand can grip and retain a living fish in water. Now the trout is up in the air and its life going in fast gulps and a frantic jerking of its tail.

This is the way of tickling trout. Before you be-come a hand at it you will have many a wetting and lose a dozen or so, but the ragged boy from the village school would make a fine teacher.

Sometimes the tickling of a trout does not end by the method of snatching. The boy or man feeling the trout will have a kitchen fork in one hand, and when the tail of the fish is within stabbing distance will thrust the fork into it and hoist the trout out of the water. I remember watching boys from the country school tickling trout when the water was low, and they caught two or three fine fish while I stood by. Fish, I was told, that had grown old and cunning, disdaining the maggot, the fly and the worm.

The blacksmith, who could hardly keep his tools in his hands on certain days when the trout were in the pool below the bridge, often went angling. When he deserted the smithy he would leave a note on the door for any farmer who called. It would state briefly, "Up the water" or "Down the water", and the caller would either go away or go up or down the water to find the smith. I remember calling with a mare that needed a set of shoes, and at the moment of my arrival the smith was padlocking his door. I tied the mare to a ring in the wall and went to him. He was going fishing, he informed me. He had a hammer in his hand and I could see no sign of a rod, or even a piece of brown line. I followed him a yard or two to the bank, where he sat down and took off his boots and socks and turned up the bottoms of his trousers.

"Come on," he said. "You might as well. The mare'll not be shod till I've done."

He had stopped the water with a dam, he told me, and now he was going fishing with a big hammer. Obediently, for I could be persuaded to any such pastime with a glance of invitation, I took off my boots and socks and waded into the stream after the smith, gasping at the coldness of the water and making grimaces of pain as I trod on a stone not so smooth as it might have been. We came to the first pool. The smith signalled to me and I stood down water from him as he indicated. He swung the heavy hammer above his head. The sinews of his wrists rose and the hammer came down with a great crash on the nearest rock. I caught my breath, for a moment later a stunned fish floated out.

"Grab it!" yelled the smith.

I grabbed and managed to get it. We waded a few paces and he struck another rock but no trout had sheltered beneath. We moved again and he struck another without result. All at once he stopped.

"Hell," he said, "look yonder!"

His landlord, carrying basket and rod, was coming up the bank. We scampered to our boots. The smith lifted his and ran over the cinders to unlock the smithy door. With the fish in my pocket, and my boots untied on my feet, I hurried after him and led the mare in to be shod. He had put on his boots and was pulling at the handle of the bellows.

"If he shows face in the door," he cursed, "I'll put a hot iron on him!"

The owner of the smithy and the stream went past and the mare was shod. I promised myself I would get down to "fish" with the smith again, but somehow the opportunity never arose.

Away in the quietness of the remote countryside there are streams where the trout are large, and safe, too, because the banks are lined with thorn and briar and gorse and straggling patches of round rushes. Here the fisherman cannot come, for the stream winds and twists like a moving snake. In such a place I learned the art of setting lines.

We had a ploughman working for us at that time, who lived in the loft above the kitchen. He slept there, clattering up the shaky wooden ladder after his supper to have a couple of draws on a cigarette butt before resting at night, clattering down in the early morning to go off before his breakfast to feed and water his horses. He asked me to come to his home with him on Sunday and spend the day wandering the rough land looking for the eggs of peewit and curlew. I had to have permission to go and I had not dared to ask up to the moment on Sunday morning after breakfast when the ploughman was washing himself at the pump. I watched him preparing himself, scrubbing his rough red hands, polishing his cramping Sunday shoes, wetting his hair and combing it down. He went up the ladder, winking at me, and I heard the sound of paper being wrapped round his bundle of washing. I screwed up my courage and asked while my grandfather was engrossed in Saturday's paper, and could hardly restrain myself when told I might go.

The ploughman's family were crofters. They ploughed and harrowed two or three acres of light stony soil away in a wilderness of round rushes, cotton grass and thorny thickets. Through this country ran the stream. Somehow the journey took away my eagerness to hunt for plover nests and cross swampy ground after the eggs of the moorhen. The ploughman's brother was on his way down to the stream to look his lines, and I went with him. Along the winding stream he had set two or three dozen. He looked round carefully before going to them, for remote as this place was, the water was "owned". Can a man own the clouds, the rain, the streams that trickle over the rocks? Can he own what the heron takes from the pool without permission, what the otter carries in his whiskered mouth? This water belonged to the owner of the land, however.

We walked the course of the stream. Half a dozen had "taken" and I could see the trout drifting at the extremity of the line. They were fine fish. This was the way to catch the really big fish, I was told. The greedy little trout was in faster water. Here each big fish had a pool or a deep stretch at a bend all to himself. Even with a rod and the right bait, such a fish was hard to catch, and all the patience a man had could be easily exhausted dangling a line. The thing to do was to put down the right worm, a red-streaked worm from the midden, one with an irresistible flavour. The trout would not look at it in the first hour. The slab of stone where the fine sandy gravel tumbled along in the current screened him from the fishing heron. His appetite was delicate. Only in the hours of darkness, perhaps the hour before dawn, would this big old trout venture to feed. He might contemplate the worm with the midden flavour for a long time before he took it, but in the end he would bite. His struggles might fray the gut before the hook but in the end he would give up. Perhaps in the cold air of the morning he would stiffen and float, or perhaps he would sink sadly down to the side of the stone and wait to be lifted out with no fight left in him.

First go to the midden's edge and dig for the red-marked, thin little worm. Gather the fog moss from a waterhole and let the worms cleanse themselves in it for a day or two. Cut pegs like those for snares and tie a couple of yards of brown line to each peg and a hook to each line. Make sure the pegs have been soil-stained or the warden will spot them. When they are ready, fill the pockets of your coat with the lines and set out for the chosen stream. Here are the places. The water ceases to ripple and goes smooth over the pot-hole. Set one here. Drive the peg right into the bank. Drop the worm-baited hook into the water. Move on a few yards. The current sweeps round the bend and flows away in under the overhanging bush. Put another in the bank here and let the bait be swept in under the bush. Walk on to the big stone. The water runs right underneath part of it, and up in the dark cold tunnel the big old fish soberly takes the water of the springs in through his mouth and lets it out through his gills. Let the line snake from the bank out over the stone so that the worm is at the entrance to the cavern. In time he may be tempted.

You must study this art. Someone else may be setting the water at the same time, someone with no more conscience than yourself. He may have an alarm ringing in his cottage half an hour earlier than yours, and when he comes down the water, having an eye for all things natural and unnatural, he may spot your setting places. Where the stream has bare, stony banks, reach into the water and lift out a big stone. Tie the brown line to this stone and put it back in the water. Leave a little indicator of some kind to remind you of the place, one stone perched on another, or a piece of dead wood among the shingle. Where the bank is fringed with undergrowth, let the line go down a branch that trails in the current. Where trees overhang, let the line drop from a low branch. On each line, close to the hook, tie a fair-sized stone, so that the hooked fish will not float to the surface and so betray the fact that lines are being set.

I can remember making long journeys at daybreak to look carefully set lines, and, making the first journey along the water I have often failed to spot my own lines. Having found the first of them, however, I usually came on the others with little difficulty. Once I arrived to disturb a heron that rose quickly and crashed at once because he had my hooked fish in his mouth, and retaining his hold on it, he rose a foot or two and was dragged out of the air. He quickly abandoned the fish and flapped off with a cry of annoyance.

The setting of lines is only one of the ways in which a poacher comes by a trout. There are many ways, and for one of them at least he will make a dam. The making of a dam is a thing for which it is best to have assistance. Put on some long boots and wade into the stream. Move the stones until they form a barrier. Add a turf or two to plug the holes, and gradually build higher until the flow is reduced to a trickle. It is a thing best done in the dry spell of early summer. When the flow is stemmed, the pools are no more than puddles and the stranded fish can be grappled for with the hands.

Two men of the village regularly sneaked off on a quiet summer's night to dam the stream, empty the pools and clear a stretch of the stream's course of big boulders so that it would be ready for netting in a week or two. The netting of a stream is a furtive process, sometimes carried out when the boys of the village are posted to watch. The net is taken by one of the poachers, who wades the water at a shallow place and sets off up the other bank, drawing to the first shallow, where the bottom is drawn in advance of the top, the catch bagged in the net and lifted clear of the stream.

When the stream is being given a rest by anglers, the poacher will make an otter, a piece of wood through which two holes are made and to which half a dozen lines are attached. The lines may be baited with wet flies, or worms or maggots, and a rope is attached to the piece of wood through the holes. Now the otter is towed out to the centre of the stream and allowed to drift under control, so that the lines are carried out on the current. Instead of one lure the fish are offered as many as they could wish, the tufted red and black butcher fly, perhaps, or the March brown with its speckled fawn and trailing hair, or the midden worm, the blue-bottle maggot, nurtured on rotten meat.

I had been keeping company with a Welsh poacher for a long time before he disclosed that he possessed a snatching hook, a gaff or cleek, as it is called elsewhere. One day, when he was showing me an old muzzle-loading gun he had inherited from his father, who had started life, like many another country boy in the old days, as a scarecrow, he looked around carefully and said, "Ever seen a snatching hook?" Like the old gun, he had had it from his father, who had had it from his own father. I felt, by the caution he displayed before mentioning the subject, that we had reached a rare intimacy. I looked at the hook. It was old and rusty. Many a fine salmon had been lifted with this hook, he whispered. Away where the river forked and came down in mare tails from the rocks of the hills, and long ago, when a day's travel had been as far as a horse could run or a man could walk, his forebears had hung about the lonely places when the salmon was running upstream to spawn. He explained how it was used. I listened, not because I had not seen one before, but because it confirmed my belief that these things were shared and had been shared by all country folk from the beginning.

The hook is four or five inches in length. It has a

shank which is hollow. The point may be barbed or it may not. In the shank there is a hole through which a strong rope is tied and the strands of the rope are bound down neatly. The rope may be five or six feet long and at its end is a loop through which a man can put his hand. The gaff is not a gaff until the poacher cuts himself a stick. As a rule the stick could be mistaken for a walking stick, a hazel rod such as any idling countryman might have in his hand when walking by the river.

Out in the deep current the salmon are crowding. The fresh current, filled with the intoxicating oxygen, the flavour of the higher land, prompts one of them to plough into the shallower water, navigate the pools and come to the fall, the place where the river breaks and tumbles over the rocks. Now the fine fish lashes its tail and throws itself at the torrent. The leap fails and it drifts back. The man among the small stones and shingle plays with his stick. The salmon tries

again and again. Now it floats back exhausted and lies in a near-at-hand pool recovering its strength, silvered and magnificent, a thing to take the breath away. The man by the water fumbles in his pocket, draws out the hook, drives his stick into the socket, pulls the rope tight so that all is firm, and looks round. In that instant he makes up his mind. The cold mountain water may swirl round his boot heads, but he will not feel its icy bite. The rod and the hook will reach out suddenly and the salmon will thresh the water as it slashes into its side. For perhaps three minutes the tug-of-war will go on. The hazel rod, no longer needed, will swim dizzily round the next pool and then come aground on the rocks. The salmon, hauled to the side and cracked on the head, will cease to struggle, and the poacher will scramble to the nearest cover to hide it or pop it into his sack.

There is such an air of innocence about the snatcher. He smokes a pipe and stares at the pools, the dark water, glinting with the glimmer of light that penetrates the screen of the overhanging fir. In Wales he might be mistaken for a rustic poet. Down the water, perched on a crag, his young son keeps watch. The fish is sold before it is caught. The hotel up the valley will hand over money at the back door. What angler could guarantee a fish for the dinner table on Sunday night?

Once I went fishing in a river, playing for a trout with a dry fly or some such lure. I stood a long time casting over a pool below a weir, sharing the water with an old man who ran out of patience too. He reeled in his line and grunted his disgust. A salmon came through the pool, making a wash like a liner. The old man suggested we went elsewhere, pointing to a small boy who played near the weir. It seemed the boy had a snatching hook and was waiting for us to go, so that we might not witness the offence. His mother kept watch from a point of vantage above the weir. We found a new pool and began casting once more. My companion tired quickly and soon left me. Curious, I went down the bank after him. I could not get near enough to find out, but I was sure he was bargaining with the mother of the salmon snatcher!

In the river where the pools are deep and channels

have been made to help the running salmon, it is not always possible for the snatcher to gaff his fish. Some of the pools may be ten or twelve feet deep and the rocks about them treacherously polished by the current, so that a man dare not risk putting his foot upon them while trying to use a hook. Here the poacher ties a great salmon fly to his line and goes fishing. He may even take out a licence so that he can have peace to do what he has to do! The salmon hovers in the deep water, gaining strength for the next stretch of his journey to the pool where the spawning will take place. The line will come snaking out, alighting on the water gently with the smallest ripple. The fly, with its large hook, will sink to the gravel and the poacher will begin to sight his fish, drawing the hook a little higher up the pool so that finally it rests a little behind the salmon. The poacher will walk a few yards and reel in so that the line is under tighter control. It is a thing needing skill and cunning. The salmon may glide a foot forward, or drift back and the poacher will have to draw in and begin again. When the line passes under and behind the fish the poacher will take a breath, tighten his grip on the rod and then whip it into the air. The hook will rise and catch in the salmon's flank, and the struggle will begin. Once the fish is pulled in, the poacher will hastily fasten a hook in the salmon's mouth, cut out the hook in its side and make off with his catch. The same method is used by poachers who draw a line across a pool and snatch the fish with a large triple-barbed sea-fishing hook.

Where the high arc of the bridge crosses the stream

a boy lies over a slab of stone, gazing, it seems, at his own reflection in the water beneath, his arms immersed to the elbow in the current, the sleeve of his ragged jersey mopping moisture unheeded. In his hands he has a noose of brass wire, a strand unravelled from a rabbit snare, straightened and remade into a new snare, a snare for a trout. Here is the skill of the greatest of anglers. He moves the snare through the water, gently, slowly, a fraction at a time, and as the noose advances the trout retreats, going back, back into the safety of the hole below the slab of stone. The boy leans out, his hair brushes the water. His eyes see only the moss green and the red dots of the trout's back and flank, the yellow tinge of the water, the small, dark stones. Now the trout has touched the stone with his tail and edges forward again. The brass wire quivers in the force of water that sweeps round the cavity. The noose is about the trout. An age passes, an age in which the boy's ears pound with the sound of his own pulses, the background noise of the flowing water. The brass wire comes nearer and nearer the gills and when it is there the boy's hands draw on the noose and the fish is caught. This is the way of the "girn" or snare, a way as skilful as tickling, as old as the spear.

The diligence of the village boy after the trout is a thing to be seen to be believed. His absorbed interest will keep him by the bank until his angry parents have become weary of calling. Without the snare or the toasting-fork spear, he will be cupping his hand to holes in the bank, careful to allow nothing to escape while he gently probes the depths of the hole with a withy wand. The probed trout will move uncomfortably and, when the stick is withdrawn, dart out to escape, and end in the grabbing hand of the boy. More than once the boy fishing in this way will find a cornered water-rat in his grasp and perhaps have his fingers nipped.

The water that ran through the quiet wood, over the stones and under the bridge, to froth and sing through the farms, is deserted by the heron and the signs of the otter are gone. Even the waterhen has deserted the banks. The fish are gone. There was a life about the place last year. It seemed that the sun kissed the water in the morning and gave it a sunset radiance before dusk. The eddies and the pools knew the motionless heron, stock-still in contemplation, the musical, stone-skipping wagtail and the life along the banks. The poachers who work on a large scale called in the half light of a summer's evening and caught all the fish, yes, like the Hamelin piper, they took every one! Up in the shallows they threw down a bag of lime and away down below the bridge they set a net across the water. Just before daylight, when all the water was discoloured, and every fish suffocated, they drew the net up. No fish escaped. The old brown trout that rose, nibbling at the drifting fly, the leaping, lively fish that threw himself in a fine curve into the sunlight, every fish, from beneath the biggest and the smallest stones, every fish came up with the net, floated and drifted against it and ended in the poachers' basket. These are the townsmen who bring mass production methods with them. For them the way of line-setting is too slow.

Two or three poachers come out to the water and set a net. They have a van parked in the shelter of the trees. Perhaps they throw a bag of lime into the stream, perhaps they buy a tin of carbide and punch a few holes in its sides, for this method works well. Perhaps they are even more impatient and use a chemical that poisons fish as well as the stream, and let providence look after the man who eats the strangely flavoured trout or salmon! When they are about, the bailiff had better stay at home, or confine himself to the activities of the cottager, or he may finish the night crawling out of a pool like a half-drowned cat.

Where the lake or the loch is in the bosom of the hills with only the shepherd's cottage in sight and the winding grey road close to the water, the "aristocrat" of poachers will come in his car. Two or three of them will unload a canvas punt and some sticks or cans of fused explosive. The hills will echo with the detonations. The quiet waters of the loch will spout upwards and subside and the poachers will row out and gather the catch with nets and gaffs. Here they will take the big lake trout, leaving the shattered corpse of the pike or the perch.

The discovery of this method seems to have been made by soldiers who bombed the rivers of France in 1914-18. It is sometimes used by poachers who have tried for a long time and without success. A fish lives in a deep pool and has scars of battle upon him, perhaps two or three flies and a worm hook in his lip. The men who know the pool have named this fish. Time has made a legend of him and the desire to hook and take him has grown hot and then changed to a desire to preserve him. Among the more desperate of the poachers is one who works in a quarry and can get hold of detonators, fuses and the like. He picks a day when the wind is high and his neighbours are about their firesides, and goes down to the pool with his cocoa tin, slow match and net.

When the men who know the pool next visit it they see the signs and know the old trout is gone. The round stones have been moved a little and a streak of colour comes from the gravel. They shake their heads and click their tongues, but they know that sooner or later this thing would have happened, even in the pool below the bridge, right in the middle of the village. There, at low water, a boy would have caught him with a snare or speared him with a fork. Perhaps he would have been caught in the shallows and stoned to death like many a fish venturing in dangerous water at a time of drought. The old trout will become a topic of conversation in the public-house for a while, and, when the thing is long enough forgotten, various braggarts will claim to have caught him with a worm or fly!

Let me show you Snib, for I cannot undertake to introduce you. Snib is a close character. He hangs about the bridge until the public-house opens in the morning. He spits tobacco juice into the river while he waits for opening time in the evening. He has very little to say. When the cormorant bobs up and dives again he watches it with detached interest. Perhaps he is making an idle bet with himself as to where it will rise, or perhaps he is absorbed in scratching the hair below his cap. He completes the scene for the visitor. There is always a man looking at a river on a sunny afternoon, watching the whorls of water, the fragments of vegetable and animal life that spin and

glide under the bridge and out towards the estuary. Snib makes the scene complete, but he does not watch the water for the bubbles and the whorls. He watches for the salmon coming up. When the tide runs out he will take note of the obstacles revealed at low water and when it is dark he will remember.

Stand close to the bar and hear him whisper, "A nice fish for to-morrow?" When he speaks of fish he means only one fish, the salmon. He and his son have a net and a boat and no conscience or love for the bailiff. In the dark Snib will remember what he saw in the afternoon, the tree branch that had bedded itself in the sand below the bend, the tangle of wire collecting weed and rubbish just at the bend. He and his son will wrap rag round the oars, put the net into the boat and paddle themselves down the water in a darkness like the crow's wing. When they are past the bend, the wire obstacle and the submerged tree, they will draw to the bank, stake down the net and then row silently across the water. Snib will feed out the net. The weighted side will sink and the other will float, supported by the corks along its edge. The running tide will belly the net and the salmon, swimming with the current, will come to the meshes. In a little while, and without more than a whisper between them, Snib and his son will row back, drawing the net in a sweep to the other bank. Snib will step ashore and his son will follow him, dropping anchor while he gives a hand. The salmon will be big enough if they are eight to twelve pounds in weight. One netting will be enough. It is a dangerous game, for there is a regulation about a licence and another about the size of the mesh of the net, as well as the number of fish that may be taken.

In the morning Snib will be at the kitchen door asking if he can have a word with the hotel keeper or his wife. Something about a salmon at twelve or thirteen shillings a pound and as fresh as the morning.

There is a way of getting salmon more often written about than used. The story books are full of daring characters who go to the river at night armed with lanterns and spears. Perhaps it happens, away in the steep banks where the river flows through the very heart of the hills, where the fir trees cling to the incline and a lantern could be hung above the water without attracting the attention of half the countryside. I know a blacksmith who made spears long ago, but he thought they were to be used for taking exhausted salmon from pools in daylight. I doubt whether an honest poacher would use such a risky method. It is like the legendary story of the irresistible salmon roe. A bit of salmon roe, they say, will get a salmon in water where no more than eels have been seen before! Where can I get the salmon roe? Who has this wonderful stuff? Perhaps it is kept with the supply of poles and lanterns that dot the course of rivers in the adventure stories of poaching. When the lantern is held over the water the salmon rises, fascinated by the light, and then the poacher thrusts with his spear. No doubt it works well enough, but the water bailiff, where is he? Hold on a minute. Make sure the indistinct form in the lantern's glow is not the reflection of the bailiff looking over the spearman's shoulder!

When you go to the trout water, or after the salmon in the river, you will have to know the bait to use. Go to the fisherman down the water and get a prawn for the salmon. The salmon, they say, does not fancy the fly, which merely irritates him, but he will snatch at the prawn. The cleansed worm will do for either trout or salmon when the colour of the spate is on the water. The boy who goes after the pike will catch a bright green frog

among the rushes, fasten it on his hook and let the
frog struggle and flounder across the water. If he
can find a mouse he will hook it well and throw it out
into the deep stretch where the pike rests. The big
fish, always ravenous, will seize it and swallow it in
one movement. Shift the stones of the ditch, arrange
and rearrange them until you isolate a little fish they
call a bull-head. You will know him. He is no bigger
than your thumb. Take him to the lake and hook
him. The pike or the sharp-finned perch will speed
for him and the line will be dragged into the
depths.

The blacksmith I knew long ago would make himself a fly. Down by the water in the evening he would
swipe at a live fly dancing above the stream and rescue
it quickly before it was carried away. With the small
feather from a sparrow or a bantam, a little bit of
coloured thread and perhaps a strand of hair, he
would wind a fly on to a hook, as neat and smart a fly
as the one that danced in the soft breeze of the evening.
This fly would be the one the trout were taking, the
one he could float on the smooth water in below the
overhanging tree. It would set up a little ripple, no
more than that caused by a thistledown moving on
a still puddle, no more than a weary fly, turning round
and round, right on the very surface of the water,
somehow making it seem thick like rich cream. Down
in the shadowed depth the trout would watch the
fly, then rise to inspect it, let it pass and suddenly spin
to snatch it down. The blacksmith would jerk the
oiled line in his fingers and tighten, taking up the
slack. By the time the trout was in his hand he would

have the recovered line already wound round his cap and the home-made fly cut from the lip of the fish. He liked to fry them on a shovel above the fire in the forge and eat them with his fingers. They were tasty this way, he said. Small ones were cooked and eaten just as they came from the water, without gutting. A trout, he maintained, was a fastidious fish and took nothing that was not clean and delicate in flavour, but I could never share this theory or his appetite. I liked to see the fish dressed with a bit of fresh butter in the frying pan!

Cycling over the hills to a river that seemed as far away as ever, a friend and I came into a valley in which stood a fine old mansion surrounded by lawns and old elm trees. Before the main windows was a lake. We stood for a while, weary of the endless ride, watching the lake. It was exposed. There was little cover between the road where we stood and the edge of the lake, but as we took our breath we thought of big carp, or pike or perch, and in a little while it became impossible to go on in search of the river. Assemble the rods and make a hasty dash across the park to the shelter of the tall rushes in the hope that some part of the swampy bank would give us access to a fishing place. We made this plan, hid our bicycles and baited our hooks. It seemed we had not been noticed from the big windows of the mansion. We reached the rushes and found an opening. The lake here was shallow. The sunlight dappled the mud and weeds. While I stared, the biggest carp I had ever imagined swam majestically through the shallows. I cast my line. The blue clay worm wriggled on the surface of the mud. The carp came on, like a fat old gentleman promenading. He seemed to pass my worm and then all at once the line was tugged and a cloud of mud discoloured the shallows. The carp had gone and my big worm with him. I drew the line out of the water in disgust and at that moment a heron flapped out of the reeds a little way along the bank. His flight was heavy and he alighted on the grass. I rushed at him, waving my rod, and he rose and made off, leaving me a handsome perch which flopped and jumped among the grass and raised his stiff dorsal fin as I seized him. The stiff fin had forced the heron to come to earth in order to make an end of his victim, but I gave the perch a nice tap on the head and put him in my bag.

We moved gradually from tree to tree, from one patch of rushes to another, until we found deep water and could fish. The finest fish of the afternoon was the one the heron caught for me. We caught several perch, but the carp kept away. Perhaps they patrolled the shallows at the far end of the lake. Perhaps we lacked the paste bait or the chicken's guts that would have attracted them. In the late afternoon we discovered an old punt moored beneath a tree and pushed off in this, hoping to get to better water. We were both fishing happily enough when we noticed a party strolling down the front lawn of the house. In our sudden panic our lines became entangled, the punt shipped several gallons of water and all our bait went overboard along with the punt pole, so that we had to pole ourselves to the bank with the rods. The group on the lawn turned out to be several young men in the company of an elder man. They were coming to swim, it seemed.

I found myself on the bank, tearing at a tangle of lines and hooks and striving to get a rod to pieces, when the first of the party reached me.

"Now you've spoilt it!" I shouted angrily. "If you are coming here to swim I'll have to go somewhere else!"

I could hardly believe my own ears. Their mouths fell open. I managed to get the tangle hacked apart and the rod taken down. With some of my longest strides I made off for the road, hurrying without too much loss of dignity, I hoped. In the village, several weeks after, I heard how some of the most impudent poachers ever had fished in the lake before the mansion, and I smiled. Legend had given us a great bag of fish, put inches on our shoulders and a belligerent air to our deportment. I remember well putting my catch to wash in the kitchen sink and seeing most of the perch, so tenacious of life, reviving and swimming round.

We went to a lake in the mountains a little later in the summer. Here, we were told, there were big lake trout, some almost as big as salmon and as old as the hills. We hired a boat from a cottage near the lake and pushed off, hopeful of a bag of lake trout. We had brought a can of maggots, flies, worms and pickled minnows. After the first few pulls on the oars the boat began to fill with water. A wind came down from the mountains and a great black cloud crawled over the lake and hung there, making the water look like pitch. The wind carried us down the lake. We had to row against the gale and bale feverishly. Only once did a fish rise and the reel whined out with neither of us able to do anything about it. The bait had dangled on the water and annoyed a trout. When a breathing spell came and we were able to wind the line in again, the hook and bait had gone. We brought the sinking boat to the shore and made our way down the track to the village, cured of a desire to catch the elusive lake trout and concluding that our lack of success had been due to the fact that we had lost our nerve and bought a licence to fish, even if we had ignored the rule about using only a dry or wet fly!

My interest in fishing began in an unorthodox manner. Willie, who used to get all the odd jobs to do, often got sent to the far end of the farm to clean ditches and streams. He would labour there in the coolness of a hollow, clearing the undergrowth, shovelling out the stones, the clumps of sweet-smelling myrtle, the white-rooted cress and the garlic-smelling weed and, as often as not, an eel or two. Some of the eels he caught were more than two feet long. I can remember how he would clamber out of the stream's bed and search the bank for an eel to chop its head off and watch its decapitated body lashing frantically. Such eels, he told me, would gash a man's palm if he dared grasp them. As a consequence of this information I was always nervous of a live eel and made a poor job of despatching it if I happened to get one on my line.

Occasionally, nearer home, where the stream widened its banks and the farm ducks swam to and fro in a kind of drill, a trout would show itself. The appearance of a trout in this bit of water was a rare thing, for the ducks, aided by an odd goose, seemed to take every weed and snail from the stream. Even my set lines were a menace, for the greedy birds were always in danger of getting themselves hooked. Here the water belonged to the rats that made their homes in the bare peaty banks and the arrogant ducks from the farmyard, until one evening I heard a disturbance down by the water. The ducks were scattering and one drake was making a pathetic noise. I hurried to the stream. The other ducks, twitching their tails nervously and making small talk among themselves, waddled off up the field in a hurry. I found the drake. He was dying, huddled in by a tuft of grass on the bank. Blood streamed from his neck. I wondered about his death for a while until an otter was taken in a trap on another stream not so far away. Until this day, apart from one trapped specimen, I have seen no more of an otter than the wash of his snout as he crossed the river at dusk.

However few were the fish in this bit of water, which in places flowed out and deserved the name of stream, and in others narrowed and became a ditch, it began my interest in fishing. Here I cornered a minnow in my cupped palms, here I watched the snaking progress of the eel, marvelling at its gracefulness in the sun-heated water. In this place I stood and stared at the waterhen taking flight with trailing feet, going hastily up to the narrows and making a little furrow in the slow current, a thing that spread out in delicate ripples and vanished before it lapped the banks. The biggest eel I ever saw moved in this stream. It came as I slumped over the wall gazing into the water, and it moved idly, waving its broad tail for all the world like the leaf of a submerged flag, except that it was brown and partly transparent, instead of opaque like the green leaf. I could have speared him with a fork, but I watched while he crossed the sun-kissed patch between a great slab of rock and a few round boulders. I was very small. It was a wonderful thing and thrilled me as only the lightning dart of a trout could thrill me after. I enjoyed the moment or two just as I later enjoyed the sight of the first brown trout I ever caught, marvelling at the beauty of its colouring, the marking of its dark back, so well matched to the bed of the stream, the shade of its under-side, cream, tea rose, honeysuckle, the shade of the belly of the stoat.

When I came to know the way of setting lines I wandered far afield to the streams that had fish in them. My aunts would sit in the early summer evenings, anxiously watching the clock and wondering if they dared tell my grandfather I was so late. Once, indeed, they made a search, imagining that they might find me head down in some deep pool, but I met them before they reached the water. I had a nice fish or two threaded on a piece of stick, but my catch went unnoticed while they foretold in angry relief the desperate end that would one day surely befall me if I persisted in such shiftless ways.

There was one place that tantalised me and attracted me to day-dream. It was a place we called the Cut, a deep gully blasted through the rock for the purpose of draining an old loch. The Cut was about fifteen to twenty feet deep and absolutely inaccessible. The water that ran through it was in summer no more than two or three feet deep. In winter it was a roaring torrent. Down in the Cut were some of the finest trout I have ever seen. I fish for them now in imagination. I like to think they have eluded others and have preserved themselves. The Cut was full of insect and vegetable life, so that these trout disdained all lures on hooks. The blackthorn, elders and hawthorns that overhung the sides of the Cut and made an impenetrable wall for the safety of cattle and small boys gave shade and cool mooring to these trout. When they tired of the shade they would come out to the middle of the stream and hover there, ignoring the morsels of food that drifted past them, just as they ignored the bait I sometimes dangled from the bridge. If I threw a pebble they would be gone, swiftly, like the blink of an eye. In a little while one would come backing downstream and another up the water to take up position there in the middle where the current had some special sweetness or warmth. In half an hour ten or a dozen would be hovering in the centre below the arch of the bridge. Visitors who came suggested all sorts of ways of catching these fine fish, but no one I knew of ever managed the feat. They may hover there to-day in the sunlight with the endless passage of the white clouds high above them.

One summer the Cut gave protection to a mallard and her brood of young. They paddled in echelon upstream. When the mother saw me she took flight and her yellow and brown mottled family hastily went into the shelter of the stone slabs, vanishing as completely as the trout sometimes did.

While we still talk of the ways of fish, of poaching trout and salmon, and in case you feel you must make a living in such a risky fashion, let me say something about the market. There is a market in salmon. Trout can almost always be sold at a fair enough price, but the poacher often keeps up the price of salmon. I know of a case of a salmon poacher who goes about his business once a fortnight. He takes his net up the water only after he has obtained orders, and he buries any extra fish he catches, or, if they are still alive after he has made his selection, he throws them back into the river. This means that he does not have to hawk fish, a shameful thing for an honest poacher, and a dangerous thing too. Other poachers have contacts in the big towns. After the night's work they will ride off to the town and send a telegram making an assignation with the retailer, who will make a special journey of perhaps seventy or eighty miles to buy the catch.

The risks are great. The penalties are heavy. It is perhaps as well to sleep soundly at nights and leave such adventures to desperate characters like Snib. The habit, once it takes, grows and absorbs a man's thoughts. Every time he finds himself in a quiet village with a stream he begins to study the water and wonder whether there are fish to be had, and his conscience about licence or ownership of water fades and vanishes like the froth churned among the stones. A man cannot be really virtuous until he has known temptation. The temptation is an old one and one which can be stirred in the most self-respecting.

I have lately taken to staying at home. Sometimes

Carte d'embarquement
Boarding pass

TKNE

Nom du passager / Name of passenger
VASEY/DOUGLASMR

De / From
STRASBOURG

A / To
AMSTERDAM

Vol / Flight	Classe	Date	Départ / Time
AF 5484	Y	16 JAN	0835

KL 2042

Enr. / Boarding

03	08H05	Siège / Seat 08F	ND

Porte / Gate   Heure / Time
NB   Poids / Weight

ECONOMY

003

AIR FRANCE SKYTEAM

Conservez ce talon.
Sa présentation est nécessaire pour
toute réclamation concernant le voyage.

www.airfrance.com

You must keep this stub.
It may be required for any claim related
to your journey.

www.campanile.com

Campanile

sur remise de ce coupon

1 petit déjeuner offert *

*1 coupon maximum par chambre et par nuit. Pour une nuit le
week-end du 01/10/06 au 28/02/07 dans les hôtels participants,
hors tarif promotionnel. Offre non cumulable.

the curlews call as they fly over at night and I think of the journeys I made across the moss. Sometimes I get a vision of a boulder-strewn river coming through a wooded valley and I feel restless. The pigeons call from the woodside on a misty autumn evening; I walk up through the hills and hear the partridge calling the covey together or the rasping note of the cock pheasant, and I curse my newly found respectability. I think of Jeck and his kind. I dream and catch my first hare again. I know that in the farmland behind the village a boy from a cottage is setting his first snare or studying the movement of the birds. I can be for ever young. Perhaps the thing with poachers is that they never grow old, at least in this one respect that they have the energy for the meandering journey to the back of beyond, the patience to shelter for two or three hours in the fringe of the wood, the capacity to become absorbed in hunting and to study all the ways of nature.

There are vagabonds among them and desperate and shiftless characters. Forget the lessons of Francie, Little Hugh, Black Bill and the rest, and let the night be a time for going to a comfortable bed.

I hope I have not disturbed you, but if ever you want to buy an old gun, a ferret, or even a well-trained dog . . .